T0305076

Sustainable Consumption, Production and Supply Chain Management

NEW HORIZONS IN OPERATIONS AND SUPPLY CHAIN MANAGEMENT

Books in the New Horizons in Operations and Supply Chain Management series make a significant, forward-thinking contribution to the study of operations and supply chain research.

Global in its approach, this series will include some of the best theoretical and empirical work looking to make an impact in research and practice. With contributions to fundamental principles, grand challenges and rigorous evaluations of existing concepts and competing theories, this series hopes to set the path for future visions in operations and supply chain management.

Sustainable Consumption, Production and Supply Chain Management

Advancing Sustainable Economic Systems

Paul Nieuwenhuis

Formerly Co-Director, Centre for Automotive Industry Research and Electric Vehicle Centre of Excellence, Cardiff University, Wales, UK

Daniel Newman

Senior Lecturer, Cardiff Law School, Cardiff University, Wales, UK

Anne Touboulic

Associate Professor in Operations Management, Nottingham University Business School, University of Nottingham, UK

NEW HORIZONS IN OPERATIONS AND SUPPLY CHAIN MANAGEMENT

Edward Elgar
PUBLISHING

Cheltenham, UK • Northampton, MA, USA

Published by
Edward Elgar Publishing Limited
The Lypiatts
15 Lansdown Road
Cheltenham
Glos GL50 2JA
UK

Edward Elgar Publishing, Inc.
William Pratt House
9 Dewey Court
Northampton
Massachusetts 01060
USA

A catalogue record for this book
is available from the British Library

Library of Congress Control Number: 2020952042

This book is available electronically in the **Elgar**online
Business subject collection
http://dx.doi.org/10.4337/9781839108044

MIX
Paper from
responsible sources
FSC® C013604

ISBN 978 1 83910 803 7 (cased)
ISBN 978 1 83910 804 4 (eBook)
Printed and bound by CPI Group (UK) Ltd, Croydon, CR0 4YY

Contents

Figures

Tables

Acknowledgements

As many authors explain in their acknowledgements, no book is the work of a single person. In our case, the combined expertise and insights of three authors allowed synergies to emerge that a single author would not be able to achieve. Overlapping expertise and experience enabled links with ideas that would otherwise be impossible. Similarly, the bouncing of ideas off fellow travellers in the same boat has been very helpful. Like others, we also see further because we 'stand on the shoulders of giants', but even 'standing on the shoulders' of those shorter of stature allows one to see further; even 'ordinary' people can often affect your thinking in extraordinary ways. In this way, many have contributed smaller ideas that have triggered new ways of looking at the problems covered in this volume. We should also, perhaps, thank those editors and reviewers who have rejected the papers we submitted to their journals and that now form the foundations of this book. By combining these, we have achieved something that could not have been achieved had those papers been published in their respective journals. That novel linking of consumption, production and supply chains might not have happened. In addition to our partners and kids, who have all contributed in their own way, a number of colleagues, former colleagues and fellow academics elsewhere deserve a mention, as they have all contributed in their own ways. These include: Maurie Cohen, Tim Cooper, Gavin Harper, Eleni Katsifou, Catrin Lämmgård, Lucy McCarthy, Jane Glover, Lee Matthews, Joe Sarkis, Diego Vazquez, Peter Wells, Lorraine Whitmarsh, Dimitrios Xenias, Natalia Yakovleva and several others.

Acknowledgments

1. Introduction to *Sustainable Consumption, Production and Supply Chain Management*

While the future of our economic system has been under increasing scrutiny for some time – particularly in the context of sustainability thinking – the Covid-19 crisis of 2020 has brought a rethink of our current practices once again to the fore. To what extent is our current way of consuming, producing and moving stuff about actually sensible and do we perhaps need to rethink all this and the way we do business, as well as the kind of businesses we run? Since the innovative but mostly overlooked work by Field and Conn (2007) carried out on behalf of the Royal Society of Arts on the topic of 'Tomorrow's Company', attempts to apply recent ecological thinking to the problems of business have remained on the margins of business academic approaches. Yet more recently, we see the existing approach to business sustainability increasingly being challenged from within the business sustainability literature itself for failing to engage with the true nature of the sustainability concept (cf. Winn and Pogutz, 2013; Hahn et al., 2017; Tregidga et al., 2018). In fact, these authors show that due to the unreceptive nature of academic journals to such, of necessity, multi- or interdisciplinary work, where it does exist, this often tends to be in book form (Tregidga et al., 2018: 321). Similarly, Field and Conn's work was not widely disseminated, for, as with many such works, it found a home in the biology literature, rather than the business literature, despite its potential relevance to the latter. This book argues, therefore, that in order to engage properly with sustainability, the sustainable business literature has to engage with the science behind it and therefore with the relevant scientific literature; but also that the very essence of ecological thinking should be internalised in business in order to facilitate a genuine, deep understanding of the place of business within natural systems, for in reality, economic activity is bounded by society, while human societies themselves are bounded by their natural environment. In this respect, then, it is essential for business disciplines to engage, at least at some level, with ecological thinking in order to play their role in any transition to a more sustainable economic system and help create the alternative business models this requires.

Attempts to link human activities with natural processes, as embodied in a broad sense by ecology, have a long history stretching at least back to Malthus (1798), yet recent advances in our understanding of natural 'systems' resulting from advances in ecology have provided a new logic to such approaches (Meadows, 2009). The aim in the brief historical sketch that follows is not for a comprehensive review of the relevant literatures, but instead to visit a selection of representative contributions dealing with the notion of linking human and natural systems over the past 200 years, as a full and comprehensive review of the relevant literature of attempts to link business disciplines with biological sciences is beyond the scope of this book. At the same time, it is important to understand why earlier attempts at integrating ecological and economic models have, mostly, failed, or, at least, have failed to capture the imagination of business academics and have thus failed to enjoy more widespread adoption. It is hoped that this – of necessity brief – overview will suffice in this respect, before advancing some new approaches to these concepts, albeit informed by more recent advances in ecological thinking.

1.1   ECOLOGY AND BUSINESS: A HISTORICAL PERSPECTIVE

In an academic sense, the crisis model of environmentalism probably started with Thomas Malthus and his work on the dangers of unrestrained population growth (Malthus, 1798). Building on this notion, economist John Stuart Mill (1848) assumed that humanity would limit consumption voluntarily to develop what we would now describe as a 'steady-state' economy within planetary boundaries, a notion later dismissed by neo-classical economists with their reliance on 'the market' to solve such problems. However, Darwin was also influenced by Malthus, thus adding legitimacy to any subsequent attempts at linking the biological sciences with the various branches of economics and business, something Nelson and Winter also use in defence of their work, adding that this provides economists 'in perpetuity' with the right to borrow ideas from biology (Nelson and Winter, 1982, 9). Notable in this period also is Engels' assertion that our perceived human victories over 'nature' will inevitably come back to haunt us (Engels, 1974).

In 1898 Veblen, in what in the present context could be seen as a landmark contribution, published an article that specifically asked the question why economics was not an 'evolutionary' science. He claimed, in fact, to be applying 'post-Darwinian' economics, claims that were contested even at the time, as explored by Hodgson (1992). His notion of evolution effectively focused on the inability of economics to recognise the development of human society in terms of 'cumulative sequence', but instead to regard it as static. This, perhaps, reflects the more limited understanding of evolution at the time (Hodgson, 1992). In reality, understanding of natural systems more generally was still quite limited around the turn of the twentieth century and many useful advances, particularly in ecology, have only occurred in the past few decades. What is significant, however, is the fact that Veblen thought the social sciences, and economics in particular, *should* look to the biological sciences for guidance and should attempt to incorporate the new scientific findings of the time into their own practices and insights. As Veblen suggested, sociology was more receptive to such ideas, thus McKenzie (1924) argued that human communities are effectively ecological entities, governed by similar processes as elsewhere in nature, although even in sociology this notion has not seen significant subsequent development. Within economics this line of thinking became more marginalised, although some aspects of the need to acknowledge natural systems were recognised at least in the 1920s by Pigou (1920) and his concept of externalities, while Gordon in the 1950s (Gordon, 1954, 1958) pointed out that unassigned property rights affect many elements of the environment, inevitably leading to market failures, which Coase (1988) attempted to solve through the idea of 'Pareto optimality' through negotiated settlements. Environmental economics was grafted onto this tradition within economics, especially resource economics, and it is thus positioned firmly within conventional economics, albeit adding to this a concern for environmental issues by, to a degree, internalising some of these externalities (de Steiguer, 2006). It should be noted that Schumpeter's (1942) notion of 'creative destruction', itself derived from Marxist thinking, also implies a – tacit – reference to biological concepts of growth and decay as part of the 'cycle of life'.

A more serious attempt at incorporating ecological ideas into economics is Nelson and Winter's (1982) concept of the evolutionary theory of the firm. These authors use the concept of evolution primarily to endow economic theory with the concept of change – something already argued for by Veblen – while also noting that companies can survive despite not maximising their activities along orthodox economic lines. This introduces the notion of apparent suboptimality, as explored further below;

nature often favours resilience over efficiency – a concept we shall be exploring in more detail at various points in the book – and thus takes quite a different approach from modern economic thinking. Although Nelson and Winter's work launched what became known as 'evolutionary economics', its impact on mainstream economics was marginal at best. A few later contributions attempted to build on this broad approach of evolutionary micro-economic notions of the evolution of firms from the perspective of industrial ecology (e.g. Nieuwenhuis and Lämmgård, 2013), although such work benefits from another two decades of work in ecology, in particular the importance of understanding ecosystems as dynamic and understanding the importance of resilience (Holling, 1986; Walker and Salt, 2006), explored further below. The concepts of Innovation Ecosystems (Jackson, 2011) and Ecology of Competition (Moore, 1993, 1997, 2006) could also be mentioned. These are further attempts to apply ecological concepts to business; thus Moore (1997), for example, argues that firms now compete through innovation and distinguishes three 'communities' in any innovation ecosystem – research, development and application – which need to be in balance for any innovation ecosystem to be sustainable. These authors see an innovation ecosystem as featuring continuous circulation of material, information and energy, just like a natural system (Moore, 1993). However, economics struggles at a quite fundamental level to recognise and incorporate the concept of limits to growth (Meadows et al., 1972), such as the 'Planetary Boundaries' concept introduced by Rockström et al. (2009). In response to this fundamental problem, Ecological Economics developed, which positions itself as a multidisciplinary field that not only forms a kind of bridge between ecology and economics, but also seeks to include links to other disciplines, such as psychology. It takes as its subject matter the totality of interactions of humans with their environment, also incorporating a historical perspective, and introduces the concept of 'social-ecological systems' (Rockström et al., 2009; Walker et al., 2002). This strand of work is the most promising thus far in integrating the science of sustainability into business academia (e.g. Whiteman et al., 2013). It is important to emphasise that the ecological approach to business is quite alien to and different from conventional business thinking and certainly very far removed from Milton Friedman's 'the business of business is business' (Friedman, 1970) which in many respects forms the foundation of the current interpretation of the economic model as it applies to business. This has come under increasing scrutiny, particularly since the 2008 recession (Denning, 2013).

Although the 'ecological' worldview (Krebs, 2008), then, is an alien perspective compared to this, yet some of its principles have already been used in younger business-related disciplines such as industrial ecology. Industrial ecology (IE) explores the interactions and relationships between industrial and ecological systems. IE is partly rooted in systems theory and has long used input–output modelling. IE aims to apply ecological principles observed in nature to industrial processes, as clarified by Shireman (2001). The concept of 'biomimicry' should also be mentioned at this point. It argues that human systems should be inspired by natural systems, but it has thus far largely been confined to areas such as engineering and design. Here structures and materials used in nature have formed the inspiration for man-made materials and structures (Benyus, 1997). One aspect of this, swarm behaviour, is developed in some detail by Miller (2010) and has already found applications in supply chain management (SCM) in the form of Ant Colony Optimisation, which brings us back to Field and Conn (2007), who were among the first to attempt to apply these principles beyond such more concrete examples to the more fundamental way in which business might operate. Attempts to make links from ecology to business may also be illustrated by Tilman's work (Tilman, 2000). He explains, for example, that one reason for the inherent stability of more diverse ecosystems is similar to the lower volatility of more diverse investment portfolios. Because species differ from each other they respond differently to environmental change. The more species this is averaged across, the less variable the total. He further argues that complex natural systems 'highlight the conceptual links between economics and ecology – disciplinary links that must be strengthened if ecological knowledge is to be used to help create a sustainable economy' (Tilman, 2000).

What we have today, then, is a landscape featuring various attempts by existing business disciplines to accommodate the sustainability agenda or to take concepts from ecology in order to apply them in some sense to business, and some hints from ecologists that their work may have relevance for business. Most of these have ultimately been unsuccessful, although some show promise. Daly (1999), himself an economist, is known for his challenges of fellow economists and of economics itself, which he would argue cannot, in its current form, deal with sustainability. Fellow economist Pearce, too, attempted to fuse ecological with economic thinking and was probably the first to suggest that we could combine economic growth with increasing sustainability (1993, Pearce et al., 1989). This was crucial in convincing much of the business community to take the environmental agenda seriously. Pearce has probably come closest to marrying the economic with the environmental, but here too the economic has tended to dominate the ecological, underlining Daly's or Krebs' argument that these are fundamentally opposed ways of understanding the world. This view also appears to be shared by Korten (1995, 1998), leaving ecological economics as the most credible avenue. However, it still presents itself essentially as a bridge between the two disciplines, ecology and economics. What if we instead integrated business conceptually as an integral part of ecological systems, which, in fact, it is in reality? This book features some – tentative – attempts to start this process of integration.

To the extent that demand drives supply – a notion we shall not leave unchallenged – the structure of this book is as follows: Part I deals with consumption and explores why it is the way it is in the developed world and why that is problematic. Part II deals with the supply side, unsustainable production, by analysing the origins of mass production, specifically of cars, to seek an explanation of why the supply side often seems to drive demand as a result of the pressure to produce to meet minimum economies of scale. In the next part, then, we explore the system that links the two, the supply chains or webs, and assess the issues it faces in taking on board the sustainability agenda. The final part will draw all this together and will draw some general conclusions and suggest ways forward, while also exploring some of the problems with current popular ways of understanding the sustainability concept itself; is 'sustainability' sustainable? Enjoy!

PART I

Unsustainable consumption

2. Sustainable consumption: an intractable problem?

The work by Denegri-Knott et al. (2018) may well come to be seen as seminal in the context of further moves towards greater sustainability. Not only do these authors highlight the contested nature of what constitutes 'sustainability', they also show how even those committed to deep green lifestyles display a fair degree of flexibility in how they interpret this concept, often favouring group cohesion over strict interpretation. Similarly, the work by Geels et al. (2015) argues for a more attenuated 'middle way' between the weaker interpretation of 'eco-efficiency' that currently dominates business and consumer responses to the sustainability agenda, which they term the 'reformist position', and the much stronger 'revolutionary position'. Instead they argue for an intermediate 'reconfiguration' position, which brings about environmentally and socially positive change within specific socio-technical systems, thereby avoiding the potentially destructive effects of revolutionary change. However, thus far, detail on what such a reconfiguration position might entail and how the necessary transition is to be achieved is lacking. It has been argued that marketing plays a unique role both in perpetuating over-consumption, and thereby the existing approach, and in potentially addressing this problem by engaging with the sustainable consumption and production (SCP) agenda (e.g. McDonagh and Prothero, 2014). These authors further suggest that this process will 'require inter-disciplinary research and engagement with other disciplines, including our colleagues in sociology, cultural studies and anthropology' (ibid., p. 1196), something suggested earlier by Kilbourne and Beckmann (1998). It is in this context that the present contribution should be seen. To explore this problematic, this book assesses the consumption problem from both sociological and philosophical perspectives by linking with some recent thinking in these disciplines, while adding to this by exploring consumption's interactions with production and, crucially, the supply chains (or 'webs') that link consumption and production.

Consumption is at the heart of contemporary capitalism, meaning that any viable alternative to capitalism will need to focus on developing a convincing argument as to how we reform and/or manage people's relationship to their 'stuff'. The capitalist system contains cracks and openings that, according to Gibson-Graham (2006), have the potential to lead to different kinds of being, which may provide us with the opportunity to glimpse and stimulate more progressive ways of relating to the products that we use. As such, developing non-capitalist subjectivities can allow people to see themselves outside capitalist social relations and thus allow a politics of the subject to counter the macro-narrative of capitalist accumulation. Growing one's own food, home manufacturing and, in particular, local, community-based decisions around how to deal with surplus through ethical trade mechanisms that curb both greed and waste, such as bartering, have become features of promoting such practices. Another opportunity to challenge the culture of accumulation, though, might be found in a more subtle means of encouraging a change in present capitalist consumption practices: buying less with the aim of keeping what we do purchase for longer. Indeed, furniture giant Ikea recently suggested that we have moved beyond 'peak stuff' and no longer wish to purchase masses of home furnishings, but rather seek to look after the ones we do buy (Ram and Milne, 2016). This pronouncement led Francis and Read (2016) to proclaim that we have reached a turning point in capitalist development, after which we shall see people 'increasingly starting to consume less, instead being content to reuse, repair and recycle what they already had'. Further indications of such a trend are networks like iFixit,[1] whose members put online guides for repairing and upgrading consumer items, such as iPhones, not designed with repair and upgradability in mind and the growing 'upcycling' and classic car movements (e.g. Nieuwenhuis, 2008). Such developments reflect the hope for dematerialisation, whereby consumers might change their intensity of use of goods and, thereon, technicians produce these goods with a lesser impact (Ausubel and Waggoner, 2008). By this line of argument, populations can grow in terms of both numbers and affluence without proportionally increasing their environmental impact. This would represent an attenuated or 'tempered capitalism'.

The concept of SCP has been attracting the interest of government and industry, as well as the UN, in the context of moves towards more sustainable societies. Yet workable solutions for the current perceived over-consumption in developed economies are proving elusive. Structural factors can be considered of some importance here, with the potential for legal and organisational change suggested by Sanne (2002), while industry is clearly also a key player in this process, as it can be considered primarily responsible for making production more sustainable (Kong et al., 2002). The links between production and consumption have enjoyed less exploration. Industry has traditionally blamed consumers for unsustainable product choices, but this view was discredited by Hart (1997). At the same time, it is hard to deny that consumers share some responsibility for their consumption and that the relationship consumers have with products and the role these play in their lifestyles is a key issue in SCP. In the context of an individual's responsibility for climate change mitigation, for example, Schwenkenbecher (2014) explored this question from a moral philosophy perspective, and surely individual consumption is linked with this, and therefore no different in this respect? She concluded that individuals, if they can be considered part of collective action, often have a moral obligation to act, even if their individual contribution is, in itself, minor. Similarly, Kohak (1985) argued that needlessly creating waste is in fact deeply immoral. In response, environmentalists have often called for 'voluntary simplification', something some individuals have been happy to adopt (Elgin and Mitchell, 1977; Etzioni, 1998; Denegri-Knott, 2018). A warning is provided in research carried out by McGouran and Prothero (2016), which indicates that although voluntary simplification may work, involuntary simplification, as tried by some of their research participants, is unlikely to last. Yet to most, such examples are of only passing interest, as consumption has become too closely associated with psychological and social factors such as identity and success, while some also allocate some of the blame to the media for promoting over-consumption (Lewis, 2013).

Whilst there are therefore many examples of studies highlighting alternative, more sustainable lifestyles, leading to more sustainable economic models, what is often lacking is an explanation of how we would move from where we are today – economies dominated by a growth model – to such more sustainable, more quality-of-life focused economic models. Where such a transition is discussed, a few different approaches emerge from the literature. Sanne (2002) for example, whose work is often referenced in this context, particularly by Nordic authors (e.g. Bly et al., 2015), advocates a much greater involvement of the state, whereby government would regulate in favour of more sustainable consumption in response to a degree of public consensus, analogous to smoking bans. Whilst this approach has some merit, it may play less well in less egalitarian and more individualistic societies, particularly those where public trust in government is less embedded. Nevertheless, Jackson also sees a role for government in a UK context (Jackson, 2006).

Another approach is advocated by adherents of the Simpler Way, such as Trainer (2014[2]). These authors envisage a transition process not unlike that proposed by the socio-technical transitions school of thought (cf. Geels, 2002; Geels et al., 2012, 2015), whereby a network of small 'niches' – within which more sustainable lifestyles are pursued – grow in number. Such niches include Transition Towns and eco-villages populated by voluntary simplifiers. In a Marxist analogy, in due course the existing system will face collapse at which time such niches then emerge as the only viable alternative and a new alternative, non-growth, regime can be built around them. In addition to analogies with socio-technical transitions theory, this approach also echoes natural processes of (eco-) systems shifting, often dramatically, from one state to another after reaching a tipping point (Walker and Salt, 2006). In such a natural transition, once marginal species may become dominant in the new system, while once dominant species can become marginal – or even disappear – in the new system. Such ecological models increasingly enjoy attempts to apply them to human systems (Winn and Pogutz, 2013; Nieuwenhuis and Lämmgård, 2013). However, it is unclear what would happen if the collapse of the existing system takes too long, or features a more gradual decline. Can society wait, or should it try and do at least something in the interim?

In line with the prevailing 'economic model' of society (Krebs, 2008), environmentalism and environmental academia have spent much effort appealing to rational behaviour, invoking 'our' impacts on 'the planet' as a result of 'our' over-consumption, or the inequity inherent in our over-consumption in relation to those less fortunate in the 'Global South'. In particular, the sustainable consumption literature has been said to have paid too much attention to consumers as rational actors (Dolan, 2002), when, really, we are looking at a practice based on deeply held ideas around perceived needs that more likely invoke subconscious desires and social positioning (Stavrakakis, 2006; Jackson, 2006; Denegri-Knott et al., 2018). Lipton and Bhaerman (2011: 33) remind us that cognitive neuroscience now holds that the self-conscious mind, only some of which can be harnessed in the pursuit of rational behaviour, represents only about 5 per cent of our cognitive activity. This means that the other 95 per cent of all our decisions, emotions, behaviours and actions are the product of the hidden subconscious part of our mind. Rational environmentalism tries to appeal to that 5 per cent, thus, not surprisingly, most of its efforts to convince us through rational argument towards more sustainable behaviours fall on deaf ears and are ignored. For this reason, otherwise perfectly rational and well-educated people may feel able, for example, to challenge the much greater specialist expertise of climate scientists in ways that they would not accept being challenged within their own disciplines or areas of expertise. Sarkis (2017) reviews some of the models psychology has used to try and deal with these limitations in the context of energy-saving options. As Lipton and Bhaerman (2011: 39) point out, this does not only impact on the individual, but it can 'alter an entire civilization' (cf. Diamond, 2005).

At first glance, then, it seems somewhat counter-intuitive, but as Neale (2008) puts it, 'sacrifice is not the answer' to tackling unsustainable consumption habits; the traditional 'puritan' approach of environmentalism is therefore an increasingly hard sell. While acknowledging that over-consumption, especially in the richer economies, offers a direct cause for our present ecological crisis, it will be impossible to motivate consumers to change by calling on them to sacrifice their luxuries for the greater good of 'the planet', despite Schwenkenbecher's (2014) argument for individual responsibility. Apart from the fact that this is never about 'saving the planet' in the first place, but always about sustaining humanity's ability to live on this planet, it seems similarly unproductive to ask the emerging consumer class of the faster-growing world economies, such as Brazil, China and India, not to aspire to the luxuries that they have seen in the established global powers. For the well-off around the world, such sacrifice is akin to philanthropy – charitable gestures to the less fortunate, representing an exercise of power directly related to the higher social status of their privileged position in society. This sacrifice would likely be limited, piecemeal and ultimately gestural. More importantly, despite their greater individual impact, it is not the small minority that constitutes the higher echelons of society who consume the most – the majority who fall into middle, service, working and 'precariat' classes are those whose combined consumption habits have the most impact. And sacrifice means something different for those with less money. Even in the UK, for example, those who have already been impacted by austerity policies, which heighten inequality and drive down the standard of living for many in an increasingly uncertain labour market with a declining role for state support, are unlikely to be receptive (Atkinson et al., 2012). They are asked to make life apparently more unpleasant again for themselves and give up on whatever slight advantages and benefits they think they are due while seeing those above them continue their lives of barely reconstructed privilege. Shorter shrift still is likely to be given to such requests by those in societies without the strong state support network or employment opportunities of the UK. The notion of sacrifice emerges as largely elitist and totally out of touch with how to gain traction with the popular opinion of the masses; we are not 'all in this together'. This highlights the notion of 'power' in this context explored by Denegri-Knott et al. (2018).

Those advocating more sustainable consumption must work with present consumption habits rather than diametrically oppose them. Mexal (2004) shows that it is important to consider notions of 'proximate space' in forwarding arguments for more environmentally sustainable practice. This means we need to make pragmatic concessions to lived experience. Dogmatism over imposing alien conditions onto people in the name of environmental idealism ignores how consumers have already built up a world that makes sense to them and which they are not likely to just abandon at the say of some 'expert'. Proposals for progressive change should be comprehensible from the current position and readily relatable to ordinary lived experience. Without properly addressing this we find the main flaw in many debates on sustainable consumption – and one that besets many ideas in the environmental activist and environmental academic worlds – that, as pointed out above, puritanism and frugality do not sell. The economic growth model has become firmly embedded during the twentieth century. Natural systems tend to work in cycles of growth and subsequent destruction, or 'degrowth', but the problem is that people and institutions do not see themselves as part of natural systems. They have developed the notion that human systems are somehow separate from other natural systems and therefore subject to a different set of – unnatural – laws. It is that which we also need to tackle. Until then we are merely trying to sell an unpalatable message. This aspect will be explored in more detail later.

Our starting point here was both the conceptual issues set out by Denegri-Knott et al. (2018) and by Geels et al. (2015). However, we combined this with the call by McDonagh and Prothero (2014: 1196) to engage with 'other disciplines, including our colleagues in sociology, cultural studies and anthropology'. In order to achieve this, it was decided to review recent literatures in these disciplines for contributions that engaged in some way with issues directly relevant to the SCP problematic, with a specific focus on consumption in the present section, particularly in the context of perceptions beyond the purely rational 'homo economicus' of neoclassical economics. In practice, this resulted in a relatively limited number of relevant articles, so the search was extended to include potentially relevant books, which also allowed a more longitudinal perspective to emerge. The resulting perspective is then used to suggest how, with some changes in approach, the fundamental principles of marketing could be used to contribute to the suggested transition to a 'reconfigured' economic system, centred on SCP. The approach taken here was therefore primarily conceptual and theoretical, rather than empirical. Further empirical work could then be considered to test some of these notions in a practical context.

NOTES

1.   www.ifixit.com/.
2.   See also: https://socialsciences.arts.unsw.edu.au/tsw.

3. Learning from the crisis

In setting out our thesis, we talked about making most of the openings that can spring up in capitalist systems, which is a notion we have taken from Gibson-Graham (2006). To follow Gibson-Graham's (2006) work, we should move away from totalising stories of how the world is, how society functions and embrace that there are other possibilities that we may not know about for certain. Across Gibson-Graham's (1996, 2006) scholarship, we are taught to imagine that the economy is constituted by a diversity of practices, which includes both market and non-market activities. It also includes individualistic and co-operative modes, motivations that can include the selfish and those predicated on caring for others.

We may be at a moment when one of these openings is emerging, with the prospect of different ways of organising and understanding our lives. In the language of Holloway (2010), we have found a 'crack'. Describing the capitalist system, he invokes imagery inspired by Edgar Allen Poe. For Holloway (2010: 8):

> We are all in a room with four walls, a floor, a ceiling and no windows or door. The room is furnished and some of us are sitting comfortably, others most definitely are not. The walls are advancing inwards gradually, sometimes slower, sometimes faster, making us all more uncomfortable, advancing all the time, threatening to crush us all to death.
> There are discussions within the room, but they are mostly about how to arrange the furniture. People do not seem to see the walls advancing. From time to time there are elections about how to place the furniture. These elections are not unimportant: they make some people more comfortable, others less so; they may even affect the speed at which the walls are moving, but they do nothing to stop their relentless advance.

This is a bleak image but his is an optimistic text, for Holloway (2010) encourages us to look for the cracks in the walls. Holloway (2010: 8) would 'run to the walls and try desperately to find cracks, or faults beneath the surface, or to create cracks by banging the walls'. He stresses looking for cracks as a practical-theoretical activity, which includes trying to create cracks through throwing ourselves against the walls but also standing back to try and see cracks in the surface.

For Holloway (2010: 8), 'a crack is the perfectly ordinary creation of a space or moment in which we assert a different type of doing'. We will not act in the way that capitalist society would expect us to and, instead, will do whatever we consider is needed or is desirable. He views this is a moment of self-determination, when we choose a new path forward.

During the First World War, while writing from prison, German Marxist Rosa Luxemburg (2004: 312) began the first chapter of *The Junius Pamphlet* with the simple but stark sentence, 'the scene has changed fundamentally'. This was a scathing indictment of the horror of war and of the economic system that had produced it. Luxemburg's (2004: 313) writing evoked her revulsion at what she saw outside the walls of her cell:

> Shamed, dishonoured, wading in blood and dripping with filth, thus capitalist society stands. Not as we usually see it, playing the roles of peace and right-eousness, of order, of philosophy, of ethics – but as a roaring beast, as an orgy of anarchy, as a pestilential breath, devastating culture and humanity – so it appears in all its hideous nakedness.

As we write this book, the scene has changed fundamentally with the rise of Covid-19. While for Luxemburg (2004: 312), what was sold by the German government as 'six weeks' march to Paris has become world drama', we have seen an illness, initially ignored as somehow just an Asian concern and, even when it came to Europe and the US, dismissed as a bad case of the flu, uproot societies across the globe. Luxemburg (2004: 312) saw that 'mass murder has become a monotonous task, and yet the final solution is not one step nearer' and we find ourselves in the middle of daily death counts where lives are reduced to rates of new infection or excess deaths. Luxemburg's (2004: 312) analysis was that 'capitalist rule is caught in its own trap, and cannot ban the spirit it has invoked' and, as we consider the system of consumption that framed and directed our lives, it feels apt to reflect on whether the consumer capitalism that dominated before the virus might not last the duration of the crisis.

War analogies are typically about machismo and cock-waving by men who have been spared the reality of suffering in wartime but want to play at being mini-Churchills (usually with the former UK Prime Minister's racism intact for good measure). We have seen it in attempts by the current holder of that role, Boris Johnson, and the like, to blunder through the Covid-19 emergency and appeal for popular support in their (in)action. Such is an appeal to heart and emotions to cover up the lack of rational thought or planning in their undercooked responses with, for example, the lack of personal protective equipment provided to NHS staff, care homes and support workers in England. We need be careful of doing the same in repurposing Luxemburg here. Her work, though, captures a sense of political, social and financial systems at the precipice, with the glimpse of something different that could be wrangled from the chaos. For Luxemburg (2004: 316):

> The World War is a turning point. It's foolish to imagine that we need only survive the war, like a rabbit waiting out the storm under a bush, in order to fall happily back into the old routine once over. World War has altered the conditions of our struggle and ... it's changed us.

So we take this quote, written in the middle of war, when the terror of this terrible, pointless fight shocked and blighted a generation, as a rejoinder that another route out of our current situation to the one that we took into it is possible. We hope Luxemburg would approve of us drawing on it here, despite the risk of patronising what those who experienced life during wartime went through, because what it speaks of is how we as humanity react to epoch-defining suffering and misery. Our current crisis means we need to work hard for whatever comes next and that means a new opportunity to do something different is little or no more work than it is to go back to how things were previously. Luxemburg's was an opening, a crack, which did not lead to the transformation she would have desired; things could be different this time.

In the UK, Booth (2020) reported that the United Nations' Special Rapporteur on extreme poverty and human rights, Philip Alston, criticised the UK government's coronavirus response as 'utterly hypocritical' due to the way successive administrations implemented policies of austerity and made massive cuts to the public sector. Globally, he noted that 'the most vulnerable have been short-changed or excluded' by official responses to the virus. For Alston, 'the policies of many states reflect a social Darwinism philosophy that prioritises the economic interests of the wealthiest while doing little for those who are hard at work providing essential services or unable to support themselves'.

We have seen the rise of eugenics back onto the political scene, especially in the response of northern European countries such as Sweden and, most visibly, in the 'herd immunity' approach that the UK government adopted early on in the crisis. This was based on the notion that it would be difficult to suppress the virus so it might be left to pass through the population to build up resistance as part of their balance between health and economic impacts. As far as the science went, the belief was that the virus kills primarily old people and people with underlying health conditions. Media commentators in the UK debated the value of the lives of the sick and the elderly and weighed these up against the widespread economic damage that would invariably be caused by stronger suppression measures. The mass of the herd that are healthy will survive, with other – supposedly weaker – members of the society being collateral to be sacrificed.

This has been the worst of what the virus has brought up, and the lack of concern for those around us is what we should fight against. There was largely a public outcry in the UK and the official herd immunity policy was quickly switched as citizens embraced the need for shielding and personal sacrifice in terms of social distancing and restricting our economic activity for those perceived more likely to be at risk. Despite issues such as an increase in casual waste from discarded facemasks and increased use of disposable items of various kinds, the virus has brought some positive factors, dim silver linings perhaps, and these are what we need to foster going forward.

What we have seen is the re-emergence of a sense of community to fill the gaps left by the state and big business as the consumer capitalist system stutters. This is the time of mutual aid. We are seeing co-operative groups springing up at street, village and town level. We have seen people use their skills to offer services that others might need such as producing the masks and gowns so vital to stemming the tide of infection for those working on the frontline. We can see the rise of local food and grocery networks, as people rediscover their community butcher or greengrocer now that visiting supermarkets is no longer the easy option it once was. Local WhatsApp groups see us check that everyone has what they need, independent shops provide essentials for those who cannot get out. And people are reassessing their priorities as social distancing and lockdown make them slow down and focus on immediate, essential needs.

Fundamentally, we have seen a growing awareness of our shared vulnerability and commensurate attempts to help each other become more resilient. This development is important and has been at the heart of an academic approach known as vulnerability theory. Fineman (2008), who has been at the forefront of the vulnerability theory movement, provides a critique of the (neo)liberal approaches to policy that dominate in Western society. Such liberal approaches are rooted in Kant's moral law, Rawls' theory of justice or Locke's liberal individualism. They assume rational autonomous individuals and take a snapshot approach to humanity that places us on our best day, when we are fit, strong, active. To be dependent, to rely on others – or the state – is considered shameful, something to be grown out of when we move beyond childhood or pitied in some patronising dismissal of a disabled person. Fineman critiques such views as assuming an invulnerability that ignores the collective experience, structural factors and imbalances of resources and power. The heart of this theory is that all human beings are vulnerable and prone to dependency, which means the state has an obligation to reduce and support citizens' vulnerability.

Fineman (2013: 21) has picked out how vulnerability is 'universal and constant when considering the general human condition' and that it 'must be simultaneously understood as particular, varied, and unique on the individual level'. She found two forms of difference – the first being 'physical: mental, intellectual, and other variations in human embodiment', and the second being 'social and constructed, resulting from the fact that individuals are situated within overlapping and complex webs of economic and institutional relationships'. Our embodiment exposes us to harm: as Fineman (2008: 8) notes, 'individuals can attempt to lessen the risk or mitigate the impact of such events, but they cannot eliminate their possibility'.

For Fineman (2008: 10), it is more likely that justice occurs if society is 'built around the recognition of the vulnerable subject'. The state should 'act to fulfil a well-defined responsibility to implement a comprehensive and just equality regime that ensures access and opportunity for all' (Fineman, 2010: 273–274). Dehaghani and Newman (2017: 1202) noted that, 'most people benefit from the state and its institutions; however, some have better access to it than others'. Everyone is vulnerable, although some people are more resilient than others. Those with better access to resources tend to have greater resilience and, in our current iteration of capitalism, that means financial capital (which carries with it additional social and cultural capital). But what if we moved towards a system where resilience was better spread to promote equity? Where the ability to accumulate masses of stuff did not matter to one's well-being and more people could have access to what they needed. Such would require a mind-shift and a cultural change. We could be in that moment.

The virus lays bare our shared vulnerability, the way we are all vulnerable but with different levels of resilience to specific threats. It has drawn out our dependence on those around us. This needs to be understood as we move forward and work out how society can be reconstituted to be more equitable. How we can move beyond individual charity and goodwill, the happy correlation of need and support that means one neighbour can help another through a particular situation, and work out how to embed the changes within our economic systems rather than this becoming like Christmas, a time of isolation when people give to charity, think about the homeless and fill food bank storerooms only to go back to business as usual once the event is over. This is a time when we are all seeing our relationships with each other and the things we consume change. We are increasingly aware of ourselves, our practices and our interconnections.

David Harvey (2020) has grasped that this moment is ripe for thinking about the construction of an alternative society. He notes:

> After all, in the midst of this emergency, we are already experimenting with alternative systems of all sorts, from the free supply of basic foods to poor neighborhoods and groups, to free medical treatments, alternative access structures through the internet, and so on. In fact, the lineaments of a new socialist society are already being laid bare – which is probably why the right wing and the capitalist class are so anxious to get us back to the status quo ante. This is a moment of opportunity to think through what an alternative might look like. This is a moment in which the possibility of an alternative actually exists.

As such, instead of instinctively reacting to the crisis by looking at how we can get back to normal as quickly as possible, we should be looking at what we did not like before, the mistakes we were making that, in part, have made this crisis worse. We should think about what we have been suddenly able to do differently when pushed to come together as a society, brought closer within our local communities, and just where this newly forged awareness of our collectivity could take us if we continued to foster and develop it.

Berry et al. (2020) have articulated that the response to this crisis needs to be grasped to avoid repeating the mistakes of the financial crisis in 2008, after which the pre-economic order was largely reintroduced. For Berry et al., 'a new understanding of economic value must become central to the purposeful and comprehensive industrial strategy now required'. They conclude that, 'while the implications of Covid-19 and a generation of economic mismanagement require an enlarged state, a progressive response must embrace also the empowerment of citizens, workers and communities'.

It is in this context that we offer our analysis on how and why we need to change our relationships to what we consume. They have already changed; we have already changed, at least temporarily. The crisis causes us to pause and reassess what is important and how we want to be. We were working with these ideas long before Covid-19 came to reshape our lives but we feel the debates are ever-more pressing considering that, as we are producing this work, so much feels transient, with a future up for grabs in a way that it may not have been just a few months before.

4. A transition phase: 'reconfiguration'

One possible way out of the perceived over-consumption culture is to think in the first instance, perhaps, of a kind of transition phase, not so much in terms of just consuming less, but consuming less but better – replacing quantity with quality, not unlike the transition position suggested by Geels et al. (2015). To give a simple example, rather than having half a dozen H&M jackets, we have one traditional Harris tweed jacket, or one from one of the sustainable fashion pioneers (Bly et al., 2015). When any of these quality items needs repair, we have them repaired and we grow with our treasured items as they grow with us. When we are done with the item, we can pass it on to the next person, provided the quality that ensures long life is there – a key prerequisite for this scenario. In addition, the social aspects of their production phase have to be addressed – a just reward and good working conditions for workers making these higher quality items have to be guaranteed, wherever they are made.

The problems surrounding mass production are explored in Part II of this book, and there are potentially difficult transitions to be made from mass production, mass consumption and mass employment to low-volume production and consumption of higher-value durable goods and consequent employment of people in higher-skilled jobs in smaller, more personalised facilities using more labour and creativity-intensive processes. Yet, with regard to consumption at least, there is significant cause to think that such an approach focusing on quality may be viable as it appeals to our basic drives to express ourselves and establish a comfortable position in society. Realigning a focus on higher-quality purchasing builds on the idea that consumption is primarily about identity construction and social status, an idea first articulated in Veblen's (1994) theory of conspicuous consumption. In post-industrial societies that produce surplus, it becomes increasingly important to consume goods that are widely accepted to be of quality in order to communicate that you are a discerning person to be respected and, as such, to establish a high place in the social hierarchy. We do not necessarily understand these motivations, but they can exert a powerful, emotionally charged effect on how we go about living our lives, such as in the decisions of what we feel we need to draw in through consumption.

The theory has been criticised by Fine and Leopold (1993) for assuming an inevitable 'trickle down' of consumption patterns from the upper echelons of society, when it is also possible for fashions to emerge from the bottom up, such as hip hop culture. At worst, then, Veblen accounts for consumption patterns that follow elite trendsetters (luxury goods) but Bourdieu's (1984) theory of distinction suggests that the ideas are of greater substance than they are often given credit for, with Allen and Anderson (1994) highlighting that they go hand-in-hand. Bourdieu's (1985) work on cultural capital refutes the idea that tastes are innate and identifies them to be socially conditioned – our habitus, or disposition, is a collection of rules, behaviours and beliefs that we subconsciously pick up and internalise from the social structures that surround us. As such, consumer choices are always shaped by the influence of the aesthetic choices of the dominant classes and represent an attempt to distinguish oneself from different, usually, lower groups. This distinction involves consumption in how we present ourselves to the world. Structural linguists such as de Saussure (1974) and anthropologist Lévi-Strauss (1974) have shown us how consumption is about an ingrained and unspoken system of signs, signifiers and signified. Building on this, Barthes (1972) picks out the mythologies that surround certain objects – meanings that draw us to them but which we do not necessarily conceive or understand on a thinking level, which need to be deconstructed in order to be comprehended. An example he gives is the Citroën DS on its launch in 1955, with the appeal of this very advanced car being greater than the sum of its parts and, more accurately, appealing to consumers by allowing them to express how modern they saw themselves to be because they were being influenced by the signs that exist under the surface of our culture (see also McCracken, 1986, 1988, 2005). By recognising and accepting the importance of purchasing, and being seen to have purchased, such objects, it seems eminently possible to work with consumers in the quest for more sustainable consumption. This approach appears much more conducive to quick yet tangible results than one based on opposing such desires to communicate and telling people not to consume. Such a perspective can be broadly located within the social practice model outlined by Spaargaren (2003), a contextual take on tackling consumerism that recognises consumption as a sociological practice to be understood as part of a wider lifestyle for the consumer.

4.1   CONSUMERISM AND CONSUMERS

For Beder (2004), the kind of traditional values such as thrift and prudence that would commonly be seen as required to encourage looking after our products over longer periods are antithetical to consumerism and can only be achieved by overthrowing capitalist consumption and agreeing to live a life based on basic levels of comfort. This might not necessarily be the case, though, and certainly represents nothing less than a long-term ambition. To foster healthier relationships with products in the short to medium term could perhaps be challenging but certainly not impossible and could constitute a key element of the closed-loop economies which some countries are now actively aiming to achieve (see also Chapter 19). It would involve latching onto, and then transforming, a pre-existing socio-cultural trend: the importance that objects of consumption have to our identity and the emotional attachment we already have to our things. The example of the car is an interesting one for the way in which the automobile can be taken to represent the height of consumerism with a firm cognitive connection established between cars and consumption (Jackson, 2006; Newman, 2013). Indeed, Alvord (2000: 21) explains how 'automobility helped usher in consumerism ... allowing the car and consumer culture to roll hand-in-hand through the rest of the twentieth century' and it seems clear that such trends persist today. To these ends, cars can be located at the heart of what Lodziak (2000) has labelled 'the ideology of consumerism' whereby the capitalist system has convinced the public to become consumers, thus instilling the mindset that consumption is an essentially fulfilling – and morally desirable – part of modern life. We do not simply need to buy new things, we have learnt to want to consume (cf. Part II). It is in such circumstances that Soron (2009) identifies the car as the foremost example of compulsory consumerism – the elevation of car ownership into a symbol of what it is to be alive today. Thus we are clearly attached to our cars; they can be important to defining who we are and what we represent (Jackson, 2006; Miller, 2001; Sheller, 2004; Nieuwenhuis, 2014).

It is possible to be highly critical of the colonisation of consumption into everyday life in this way. Notably, Debord (1995: 16) argues that, in 'the present phase of total occupation of social life by the accumulated results of the economy', we have declined from 'being' to just 'having'.

Debord is important as he inverted Marx's understanding of the functioning of the economy, updating the relationships between the base and superstructure to highlight that, today, consumption and not production is the main driver of capitalist society. Thus, we experience life as an accumulation of spectacles to consume in the illusion of constructing an identity and need to wake up to what our authentic needs actually are – free from capitalist influence. This is easier said than done; Baudrillard (1981) identifies that there is no way of distinguishing between 'true' and 'false' needs and that the consumer is involved in constructing identity. While Baudrillard accepts Debord's thesis that there is now a primacy of consumption and considers that in advanced capitalism we have become compelled to surround ourselves with objects as much as we do other people, he takes a different line on the consequences. He rejects the reduction of needs to simple utilitarian use value and, rather, posits that needs are socially constructed. As such, there can be no innate property of what is legitimately needed, rooted at the bottom of society, but only a flexible and changing conception that is led by social actors and the values they attribute to objects through interaction. For Baudrillard (1981), there are four value-making processes: the functional value (the instrumental purpose of what a thing does); the exchange value (an economic measure of relative worth); the symbolic value (assigned by a subject to an object to communicate with another subject), and the sign value (the place of one object within a wider system of objects, a semiotic communication). Credit is duly given to the consumer to exert their own influence in establishing need – values are not simply handed down from on high but are negotiated in practice. This is useful, as Jackson (2006) too sees one of the barriers to more sustainable consumption as vested interests from marketers, advertisers and retailers in perpetuating existing patterns of over-consumption.

While Debord's negative approach to the dominance of consumerism could be used to take the well-worn Marxian line of considering consumers as cultural dupes, the post-structuralist unpicking of Baudrillard is more even-handed and gives consumers greater credit. Signs of consumer resistance, as exemplified by the 'freedom to tinker' (Franz, 2005) or consumer 'pathologies', such as an interest in obsolete products (Nieuwenhuis, 2008) could therefore be considered positive. Crucially, with regard to the idea of fostering a more sustainable emotional relationship to objects, Baudrillard carries far more potential for positive change within the current system than relying on convincing consumers to give it up. Consumers, then, are not to be understood as passive victims but can be taken as active participants able to exert some level of control over the process of identity construction that occurs through capitalist consumer practices. Such is the approach advocated by Todd, who highlights that consumerism must be seen as social rather than merely economic (Todd, 2012: 50):

> While it is easy to conclude the consumption of products leads us to develop a sense of who we are as a person, it actually does much more than that. Consumerism helps us figure out where we fit within society and provides the means by which to change social circumstances. It is easy to disregard consumerism as shallow and devoid of meaning ... However, if you choose to be a consumer and accept identity and social circumstance is a construction there is a sense of liberation. Consumerism hands us the tools to become whomever we want and lets us make the decision on how the world views us. By acknowledging we are not defined by what we own we can look consumerism in the eye and say 'this is what I am because I chose it'.

Jackson (2006) also argues for a degree of control on the part of consumers in shaping the meaning of symbolic resources. It is here that he sees scope for government intervention. This is a hopeful message that consumerism need not be accepted as owning us and neither should capitalist practices of consumption be construed as inherently negative. We are reminded that there are all manner of possibilities for change under the present system – the unhealthy practices that exist in consumer capitalism can be subverted from within when we do not assume that the system controls the individual. De Angelis (2007) has documented how dominant capitalist practices can be reformulated in more sustainable ways within the current socio-economic system – revolutionary spaces can always be forged by choosing to perform certain practices in different ways. A more sophisticated and thoughtful approach to consumption can be accommodated within the capitalist system as at least some manner of growth might still be attained through the purchasing of a smaller number of higher-value goods over a larger number of cheaper products (while changes in self-identity over the lifespan ensure there will still be ongoing demand for new goods). The importance of consumed products such as cars to our identity can be used to appeal to consumers to make sure they appreciate their purchase – if it means that much to them, surely such a positive attitude to looking after the goods can also be developed. Moving back to the view of observers like Sanne (2002) and Jackson (2006) that there is a role for government in nudging consumers towards more sustainable consumption patterns, what form would such policy interventions take? What interventions there have been have not been very successful, except in the case of tobacco.

5. Consumption and our place in nature

The suggestion here is, therefore, not for the austerity of reduced consumption as such, but for an intermediate phase of consumption of fewer, higher-value, more-durable goods. Once we get to this intermediate consumption stage – or ideally much earlier than that – we can then begin to tackle the more fundamental question of our place vis-à-vis what we call 'nature'; a term that is itself misleading in that it already separates us from the rest of life on Earth. As suggested by Morton (2010), the term 'nature' should be abandoned in order to come to a more fundamental understanding of how humanity relates to the rest of the planet, the impact of its actions and the feedback loops that will inevitably come back to haunt those who push systems too far (Walker and Salt, 2006). It is this higher-level thinking about the place of humankind in the world that seems to be lacking in much of the environmental literature, as perhaps exemplified by the 'degrowth' literature (Georgescu-Roegen et al., 1979 and subsequent work; Kallis et al., 2012, Ashford, 2016), which is discussed in more detail in Section 5.1, below. Many such works are still perhaps too closely linked conceptually with an economic rather than an ecological mindset (Krebs, 2008). This failing is of course shared by the marketing literature and the literatures of most other business disciplines. Walker and Salt (2006) explain that natural systems can achieve equilibrium in various different states, each of varying stability. Some of these are more suited to humans than others and these are therefore more desirable; they ensure or facilitate human survival or comfort through the extent to which they can provide 'ecosystem services' to humans. However, the system, or indeed 'the planet' can exist in any of these states; any of these can be stable in its own way. Humans therefore very often seek to stabilise a particular natural state because it brings those ecosystem benefits they are after, including the exercising of our need for technology such as agriculture. Even when protecting nature, humanity is therefore shaping it. In reality, humans have become totally intertwined with their technology in the broadest sense, such that humans and their technology combined constitute our species. To a large extent we have co-evolved with our technologies – we make them to suit us and we adapt to them such that we increasingly suit them (Spyker, 2007). For example, our control of fire allowed us to keep predators at bay, change our environment and cook our food (Lipton and Bhaerman, 2011). Similarly, our stone tools did a job for us and then we adapted to become better at making and using them (Reardon, 2013). The human relationship with objects has therefore become of crucial importance and yet is in some respects not fully understood. On an ethical level, Kohak (1985: 35–36) explored the intrinsic value and humanity's inherent moral obligations towards its artefacts:

> Artifacts are not only products but also gifts, be it of God or of Nature. Their being has been bought at a price, be it of animals slaughtered, trees felled, ore mined. A gift, though, requires gratitude as a response. It is surely one of the most elementary prima facie obligations to treat a gift with respect ... It might, to be sure, sound farfetched to speak of my moral obligation to an aluminum beer can discarded by the road side, yet that obligation is real. That aluminum, embodying both a prodigious amount of labor and a part of God's creation – or, in a secular metaphor, a non-renewable natural resource, is a gift. Though it might be my privilege to use that resource, that gift, it is immoral for me to waste it.

It is even possible that technology is used as part of the human role in natural systems; nature would then use our technological aptitudes to help it in its efforts to achieve equilibrium in the natural systems of which we are part. This is still speculative, although Lipton and Bhaerman (2011: 209) argue that 'Humans, like every other organism in the biosphere, are here to support environmental balance, to buffer it, to sustain it, and to encourage harmony.' Humanity is not, therefore, as some 'deep' greens argue, a blot on the landscape causing only harm and no good. Lipton and Bhaerman add, like Field and Conn (2007), that we are unique in our awareness of our evolution and of our potential for change; we can therefore gain awareness of our role in maintaining harmony in natural systems and act accordingly. As part of this approach, we also need to change our relationship with the objects around us. For example, we need to start looking at objects as part of systems, rather than single entities, an approach to which cars lend themselves particularly well (Nieuwenhuis, 2014). Cars are themselves made up of more than 20,000 components all working – ideally – in harmony to deliver us personal mobility, identity, enjoyment, while they are part of a system of conception, production, distribution and use that all contribute to the very complex system of 'automobility', or the automotive 'regime' (Wells et al., 2012). As Jackson (2006) argues: 'There are few places where the symbolic character of material consumption is more naked to the popular scrutiny than in the case of the automobile', thereby directly linking the human with the object. In this sense, an ecosystem approach is like systems theory (Meadows, 2009), while the car has become, perhaps, the archetypal mass-produced consumer product.

5.1   DEGROWTH

It is not possible to discuss the concept of degrowth without first considering growth and the way in which economic growth has become the dominant social imaginary of our age (Castoriadis, 2010). In other parts of this book we explore our modes of production and consumption and how the constant desire for and production of ever more and newer 'things' – ideally cheap – is one of the primary drivers of the unsustainability of our entire economic system. The growth paradigm is not only deeply embedded within our modes of organising our production and consumption systems, it has become deeply engrained into people's mindsets (Göpel, 2016). The inescapability of the growth discourse makes thinking about alternatives challenging, given that 'Economic growth is organised around and shapes a range of tightly coupled structures, including institutions, norms, discourses, culture, technologies, competences, identities, etc.' (Büchs and Koch, 2019: 160).

The growth lock-in we find ourselves in is by no means an objective or 'natural' occurrence. Instead it is a political choice and has resulted from decisions and actions that were made and taken in specific context, during which growth was seen as a politically desirable way to address the economic and social problems of that context, including the social instability and unemployment associated with the Great Depression, and the necessity to organise the war response in the Second World War and the Cold War (Barry, 2020). The ideology of economic growth has been promoted and sustained through the discourse of international organisations such as the World Bank and the Organisation for Economic Co-operation and Development (OECD). Indicators such as GDP are constantly used in the public narrative in order to describe the health of an economy and to distinguish between nations that *do well* and those that do not. Interestingly the very framing of indicators like GDP shows the tight association between concepts of productivity, value and the idea of growth. What is not measured is not productive and hence not valued, and *resources* must be mobilised, made productive to ensure growth (Barry, 2020). The fact that our key measure of national economic growth, GDP, ignores key natural human activities, such as caring, because they are non-salaried and therefore *unproductive,* already shows how unnatural our current conceptualisation of the economy is. Economic growth has become the one way to legitimise the commodified organising of our activities. The endless growth imperative has colonised all spheres and we witness this through the promotion of endless growth across all institutions, including the third sector, such as universities where aggressive growth strategies trump all other objectives.

It is important to note here that the issue is not with the idea of growth in itself. In fact, all organisms on Earth grow and growth is a natural phenomenon. As humans we grow from being babies to full adults; trees and flowers grow from seeds, etc. What is problematic, however, is the very notion that growth *should* be limitless, and this is indeed the very idea that iconic publications such as the *Limits to Growth* report (Meadows et al., 1972) picked up on. The natural phenomenon of growth has limits; things grow until they reach a mature and stable state before falling into decline or decay. New things take over and follow a similar cycle of life, growth and death. The very idea that economic growth can be endless is unnatural and counter-intuitive. Yet it is a successful 'myth' which we cling onto (Jackson, 2009) because its main promise is that of social progress or development, which here is viewed as encompassing wealth, well-being, etc. Yet what can be seen is that the means – growth – has become the end and we have stopped interrogating our perpetual search for more and our support of the growing economy. The question 'Why do we need to grow?' is seldom asked (Barry, 2020) and it is instead taken for granted not only as an imperative for nations but also for both the public and private organisations that make them up. These conditions make the idea of endless economic growth seem inevitable; Büchs and Koch (2019: 50) summarise the pervasiveness of economic growth eloquently:

> From this perspective, economic growth is not just an external premise that actors can decide to act upon or not, but it is a principle with structural properties that is engrained in ways of thinking and acting – for the most part habitually. Growth thus becomes something that is perceived as 'natural' by the vast majority of actors. A range of scholars have argued that the growth paradigm is deeply embedded in people's minds and bodies (Göpel, 2016; Lane, 1991; Welzer, 2011; Büchs & Koch, 2017: ch. 6). This implies that people's iden-

tities and life goals are closely aligned with the idea of growth – shaped by ideas of social progress, personal status and success through careers, rising income and consumption. Even seemingly alternative goals such as 'personal fulfilment' can be infused with ideas that remain tied to the growth paradigm, for instance if fulfilment is sought through high consumption and high emissions practices such as extensive long haul travel or expensive hobbies and gadgets. As Meadows (1999) has pointed out, the most effective, but also the most difficult step in system transformation is the shift of paradigms that underpin the system. Again, since this is difficult to influence politically, it presents a major hurdle for a departure from growth-based systems that also maintains wellbeing.

The legitimacy of endless economic growth is ensured and nurtured by a discourse of strict separation of humanity versus nature, which we challenge throughout this book. The implications for the organising of our production and consumption systems are immense. The endless growth ideology commodifies everything, from the workforce to the very organisations they are supposed to serve. We can blindly exploit natural resources to serve the growing economy, which is itself conceived and legitimised as serving human consumption. Consumption and serving the *free-choosing* consumers are central justifications to the imaginary of endless growth. Humans are often reduced to their identities as consumers and their freedom is constructed through the very act of consumption. How many times do we hear 'we do it because this is what the consumers want'? In order to maintain this strong illusion of autonomy and agency, consumption must be encouraged and promoted, in particular through the creation of ever-more wants and desires, which in turn results in more consumer goods being produced to sustain ever-growing businesses. This is the virtual cycle between endless economic growth, and our consumption and production systems. The latter do no longer exist to satisfy important human needs but to prop up the capital-exploiting and -accumulating economy. Global production and consumption systems are orchestrated by large Western multinational corporations, which operate through geographically dispersed and increasingly fragmented supply chains. These systems serve the Western values of cheap and ever-more consumption and are grounded on the exploitation of labour and natural resources, especially from the Global South. People and resources are only valuable as far as they can contribute to sustain the growing corporations. Under the endless growth ideology, bigger is always better and the quest for efficiency is paramount. As we continue to rely on ever-more geographically dispersed and fragmented production, it becomes more difficult to trace full supply chains and maintain visibility (Dicken, 2007). We become more and more detached from the provenance of our consumption goods and hence emotionally distant. And the question of 'Who does the dominant paradigm of endless growth actually serve?' becomes ever-more relevant. Certainly not people and/or natural resources. As Barry (2020: 2) puts it:

> What if economic growth is simply an idea that serves the interests of a minority in society rather than being of benefit to everyone? What if the 'social imaginary' of endless growth (Castoriadis, 1991, 184), is a ruling idea of our age because it is the idea of the ruling class? And serves that class's interests by becoming a 'core state imperative', but is not, after a threshold or as a permanent feature of the economy, in the long-term interests of the majority in society, future generations or the non-human world? Viewing growth as the ideology of the ruling class or elite means to understand that since the main aim of an elite ideology is to maintain the hegemony and power of this elite, issues of its ecological irrationality (or indeed social and economic irrationality) are unimportant.

Yet the ecological danger and socio-economic downsides of the elitist pursuit of endless economic growth are not unchallenged and the voices against it have multiplied and become louder. Arguably the current pandemic has contributed to exposing the cracks in the system, shedding light on deeply entrenched societal inequalities as clear evidence that the promises of endless growth are far from having materialised.

It is in this context that the idea and socio-political movement of degrowth takes its full meaning. Here we would like to build on Latouche's view (2009) that degrowth does not equate to negative growth, which is an oxymoron, but is about breaking away from the ideology of endless growth and our addiction to productivism.

> Strictly speaking, we should be talking at the theoretical level of 'a-growth', in the sense in which we speak of 'a-theism', rather than 'de-growth'. And we do indeed have to abandon a faith or a religion ... and reject the irrational and quasi-idolatrous cult of growth for growth's sake. (Latouche, 2009: 8)

The degrowth movement find its roots in ecological economics and has been around for quite some time, but its practical translation and implementation remain at best elusive. The purpose here is not to go over the entire degrowth debate. Research contributions on degrowth are abundant and excellent reviews and summaries have been provided by scholars such as Demaria and colleagues (2013) and Kallis and colleagues (2018).

It is valuable, however, to consider some of the main aspects at the heart of the degrowth conversation, in particular the topic of the economy's relationship to nature, diversity and smallness, and technology.

As mentioned previously, growth is a natural process, which naturally precedes stability and decay. As such it is unsurprising that many of the arguments from the degrowth literature can be viewed as the establishment and growth of more equitable and just institutions or local eco-friendly initiatives which can contribute to increased community cohesion and well-being. For example, one can imagine the benefits of *growing* access to universal health care. At the very heart of this is the return to what economic growth was promising to offer and failed to deliver: well-being and prosperity for all. Some argue that degrowth is a perspective of abundance (Hickel, 2019) rather than scarcity as many of its critiques would like to label it. The ecological underpinning of degrowth also requires thinking about what this means within our ecological limits, and fundamentally acknowledging the ecological debt of the Global North to the Global South (Latouche, 2009). Degrowth and post-growth economy imaginings are thus all based on the re-imagined relationship between humanity and nature and have a strong ethical foundation (Schneider et al., 2010). What values underpin consumption and production in a prosperous post-growth world? How do our production and consumption systems need to be governed in this context? If we detach ourselves from the ideology of endless growth and accept the natural cycle of life, how can this help us conceive new ways of organising and new business models?

A number of theories exist as to what a degrowth world economy would look like, some more established than others. Steady-state (Daly, 1996) and flourishing (Ehrenfeld and Hoffman, 2013) are examples of such conceptualisations. Latouche (2009: 33–43) proposes that 'virtual circles' of eight interdependent changes must be actioned to achieve an 'autonomous degrowth society'. This is what he calls the eight Rs: 're-evaluate, reconceptualise, restructure, redistribute, relocalise, re-use and recycle'. His argument is one that resonates with several of the ones put forth in this book, in particular in Part IV. Re-imagining production and consumption systems through the lens of Latouche's eight Rs puts into question the very existence of large corporations and their globalised supply chains as the dominant mode of governance of these systems. Localism, smallness and diversity are central to the degrowth imaginary and this is where we find the strongest articulation of a perspective where humanity and all its activities are seen as embedded in nature and not separate from it. Indeed, smallness and diversity are key features of ecological systems, as we discuss later in Part III of the book. Hence degrowth would support production and consumption ecosystems that like other ecosystems function and thrive because of the interdependence between the diverse species and organisms within them. The species within the system reap benefits that are both material and non-material; they are able to fulfil their physical as well as emotional and social needs.

The reconceptualisation of production and consumption as ecosystems also enables interrogating and re-imagining the place and role of technology within them. The endless growth ideology goes hand-in-hand with a vision of technology as salvation, in the sense that technology enables the fixing of all 'problems': economic, environmental and social. This articulation of technology is deeply rooted in a strict separation of humanity and nature, whereby technology enables control and power over the non-human world, turning everything into objects (Kallis et al., 2018; Acquier, 2019). Like growth, one can view the obsession with technology as a confusion between means and ends. Much funding is poured into the development of new technologies – techno-fixes? – with little interrogation as to their broader purpose. We pursue technology for technology's sake, it is ever-expanding and alienating (Acquier, 2019). It is of course embedded in and reproduces our deeply inequitable and eco-logically damaging socio-economic system, and questions arise as to who benefits from the development of technology. The degrowth literature has little on technology as such, but it is possible to see the emergence of some post-growth imaginings for socio-technological systems as well as already existing applications (see Kallis et al., 2018). They exhibit a shared vision for technology: it is local, communal, adaptable and slow.

Figure 5.1 is an attempt to illustrate the fundamental difference between economic systems under the endless growth paradigm at the top and the degrowth movement, as articulated above, at the bottom. Whilst the former is based on the premise of eternal economic growth at the expense of the ecological world and beyond the natural carrying capacity of the planet, the latter can allow for a reconnection between the ecological and economic systems.

Detaching ourselves from the growth ideology enables surfacing not only the deeply rooted issues with our existing (over)production and (over)consumption systems but also the possibilities for reconceptualis-ing them. In particular, it fundamentally reshapes the very notion of con-sumption towards a more eco-centric, less materialistic, non-alienating

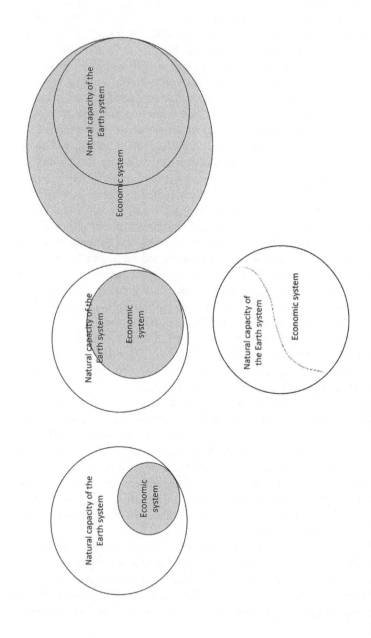

Figure 5.1   Economic systems: growth versus degrowth

view where the relationships between humans, their needs and objects that fulfil them are transformed.

5.2   SHAPING OUR ENVIRONMENT AND OUR THINGS

It has been argued that one of the causes of premature disposal of things lies in the inability of those things to grow with us (Chapman, 2005) and this includes our growing inability to adapt those things to our lives. It is natural for us to want to influence or change our environment. In this context, to be presented with a product that discourages input from us is, in a very real sense, unnatural. For centuries, people maintained, repaired and modified their objects and many examples survive in people's homes, antique shops and museums. In the early years of the car, such input was normal (Franz, 2005; Nieuwenhuis, 2014). While Crawford (2009) explores the benefits for us as humans to maintain a balance between such manual and mental activities, Franz (2005: 130) concludes that, under the new culture that developed gradually during the 1920s and 1930s, with the rise of mass production:

> ... in the eyes of the industry the perfect consumer did not tinker, but rather told the manufacturer what he or she wanted and then waited to receive the benefits of the 'holy trinity' of the modern age: science, industry and progress.

This is a model we are still familiar with today and which is responsible for the loss of that close human–object relationship that could help ensure more sustainable consumption (Spyker, 2007). But leaving this to a technological elite divorces us from that important and inherently human bond with our technologies. Assuming that premature disposal is wasteful, or indeed even morally questionable, as Kohak (1985) has argued, is it possible, then, to make consumers more attached to their objects and thereby reduce this waste burden? The longer a product lasts, the less often it needs to be replaced, and therefore the less often it needs to be produced, thus reducing overall production and resource use. At the same time, durable products significantly change patterns of consumption (Cooper, 2005, 2010; Nieuwenhuis, 1994, 2008, 2014). Yet, products are often discarded not because of a lack of technical durability, but because the consumer has lost his or her emotional attachment to them (Chapman, 2005; Muis, 2006). At the same time, products built for an expected lifespan of only 10–12 years, such as many cars from the 1960s, can be made to last many decades, if an owner can be found who is willing to build an emotional relationship with the product (Nieuwenhuis, 2008, 2014) and if policies, regulation and marketing are used to encourage such approaches. By exploring this type of relationship, it may be possible to discover just how it could be used to build a model for sustainable consumption. Chapman (2005) argues that in most modern consumer societies, most products are discarded because the owner has 'fallen out of love' with the object. As a result, waste sites are full of working machines and serviceable objects. Chapman (2005: 9) blames the prevailing industrial model, explored in Part II of this book, for this system of consumption: 'consumers of the 1900s were not born wasteful, they were trained to be so by sales-hungry teachings of a handful of industries bent on market domination'. One of these industries is the mass-production car industry, particularly General Motors under Sloan.

6.   A new role for marketing?

McDonagh and Prothero (2014: 1201) remind us that current marketing philosophy is centred on the concept of 'creating consumer value'. This is actually a surprisingly broad notion, which provides considerable scope for expansion and reorientation. In the present context, for example, it could be argued that a clean and sustainable environment is of at least equal value to citizens, as consumers, as any product or service they may wish to acquire or use. Why then, is this aspect of 'consumer value' generally overlooked? The disconnect here is with the conventional, limited view of marketing as focused on the promotion of specific goods and services. However, by moving those same general principles to a higher level, they could easily be applied to issues of sustainability, even of sustainable consumption. But it is precisely here that the disconnect is most pertinent, as one view seeks greater consumption while the higher-level view would generally aim at dissuading greater consumption in the conventional sense. Kilbourne and Beckmann (1998) also note this failure to consider the higher-level, 'macro' relationship between marketing and nature.

But given its existing priorities, how could the marketing discipline contribute to this agenda? Once we consider the consumer as also a citizen and a member of society, surely a clean, healthy and sustainable environment, both natural and cultural – if such a distinction indeed exists (see above) – would create considerable value to that same consumer. It is precisely in this area that marketing could play a role. Rather than a narrow focus on conventional products and services within a mainstream economic perspective, here it is argued that a broadening of the scope of marketing to move beyond the economic realm into the wider social and environmental realms is not only possible, but long overdue. An intermediate transition phase – e.g. the reconfiguration of Geels et al. (2015) – whereby the use of longer-lasting products is promoted, would still offer opportunities for conventional marketing approaches as such products could be remarketed from one user to the next, while marketing at the higher level could then be used to help guide the transition from an economic to an ecological model. In both areas, then, marketing has a role to play. In fact, Belz and Peattie (2012) propose a widening of the marketing agenda whereby it deals with both markets and society in a broader sense, which includes the environment, and with a much greater emphasis on relationships. Further, Hartman and Apaolaza-Ibáñez's (2013) research points towards a role for including what they term 'natural environments and imagery' in advertising as a means to stimulate the consumer. It seems a logical step to move from simply using this idea of nature as a general background to sell products towards utilising such themes of nature and our integration with it as a specific marketing theme.

Daub and Ergenzinger (2005) propose the notion of the 'generalised customer'. To think of people merely as consumers or customers captures only a part of a person's multiple roles in society. While someone is a consumer, he/she is at the same time a citizen, parent, trade union member, member of a pressure group, employee or employer, etc. So why does marketing preoccupy itself with such a narrow aspect of the individual? Does it not therefore make sense for marketing to attempt to engage on this much broader front and deal with people in all those aspects? This would automatically involve it in a much stronger social and environmental set of activities. Daub and Ergenzinger base their concept of the 'generalised customer' on Mead's concept of the 'generalised other' (Mead, 1934; Dodds et al., 1997; Holdsworth and Morgan, 2007), which refers to the way individuals are linked to their wider group, something also highlighted by Denegri-Knott et al. (2018). Thus the community or social group that gives an individual his or her unity of self can be called 'the generalised other'; the attitudes of the generalised other are the attitudes of the community as a whole. The community exerts control over the individual through the generalised other, while the thinking of the individual reflects that generalised other.

Thus customers are also stakeholders, often potentially critical stakeholders in relation to those very businesses that may try to sell them goods and services as mere customers or consumers. Recognition of this fact could help lift marketing to that higher level, whereby it could still play its role in promoting goods and services, but in addition it would seek to interface, or indeed build relationships with generalised customers in all their other aspects, including addressing their needs as an integral part of wider social and environmental systems. In fact, Daub and Ergenzinger (2005) suggest that such a change would feed back into production and service delivery processes and force these to also consider wider social and environmental concerns in their activities. More sustainable products and services would need to be offered to satisfy the generalised customer, rather than the current perception of addressing these only to a partial 'customer'.

Follows and Jobber (2000) have shown that marketing must take sustainability seriously, as the criteria used by consumers to evaluate products have changed. Consumers increasingly consider the long-term environmental – and social – consequences of products before making their purchase decisions; though they do so only as part of an evaluation that also considers short- to medium-term personal implications to the consumer. In modelling environmentally responsible purchase behaviour, Follows and Jobber found that, while negative environmental consequences can disincline consumers to purchase a product, environmentally advantageous products must not be felt to leave the individual consumer at a disadvantage. Sustainable consumption, then, is marketable but involves a hard sell that requires a product that can be felt to benefit both the environment and the consumer.

Recent research looking at consumers' goals that influence the consumption of environmentally sustainable products has considered intergenerational justice, environmental equity, self-esteem, transcendence and continued existence (Ramirez et al., 2015). Such goals vary in their level of abstraction, involving a range of short-, medium- and long-term motivations united by a core sense of working for some sense of justice and standing against injustice. Ethical consumption can be considered a form of individual empowerment that, with the growing buying power of many consumers, suggests some groups of consumers might have little tolerance for products that are not deemed to be responsible (Shaw et al., 2006). While recognising Rivera-Camino's (2007) findings that stakeholders influence organisational green marketing strategies in a non-linear and piecemeal fashion, such a view could mean that consumers are considered able to take on roles as active citizens in search of fair and ethical product choices and services, thus participating in the marketplace. This suggests the need for an approach on the supply side that offers innovation and responsive options.

7. Unsustainable consumption: conclusions

Telling people to stop consuming will not work; a close relationship with objects has become an inherently human characteristic, it is part of human nature and any attempt to break this will likely bring about an antagonistic reaction towards the environmental cause as consumers fight to defend their right to buy and enact their need to find a personality and social standing they are happy with. More realistic, then, to encourage a more self-aware consumer and more 'reflexive' consumption practices. These would encourage consumers to think about themselves as part of a broader system – the reflexive generalised customer – to think of the reasons why they are consuming, prompting them to reflect on what it is they hope to gain and how they can fulfil that need. If consumerism is about purchasing for social status and self-identity, consumers should understand these motivations and marketing should play a role in enhancing this deeper understanding.

The present trend does seem to be for consumption patterns based primarily on relentless accumulation, as we feel compelled to buy more and more in order to gain the satisfying life promised by consumerism, its media and its marketing. We engage in Kaplow's (2009) desperate 'hoarding' activities because we cannot find what we need. But maybe we do this because we do not know or fully appreciate what the consumption process is – how it involves far more than just buying products when we are actually buying our 'selves'. More sustainable practices of consumption, then, might be premised on encouraging consumers to buy what they really want – not simply stuff but the right thing for them at that moment in their lives. This implies a new 'higher' role for marketing which would involve it in activities and approaches that could contribute to a process of using less but better, which seems far more realistic than demanding that consumers use less, full stop – this is progressive reconfiguration rather than outright revolution. The impact of such a change in approach could be crucial in allowing a way into reduced consumption and the resultant environmental benefits that would follow. Such 'mindful consumption' can act to curb the worst excesses of consumer capitalism while allowing us to retain our ability to buy the products we most desire and then adapt them while we live with them over a longer product lifespan.

The main issue addressed here is the possible pathways that a transition from the current growth model in consumption to a more sustainable model of consumption, informed increasingly by aspects of quality of life, could take and, in the current chapter, particularly the role marketing could play in this. The literature presents us with two possible models, to which this analysis adds a third. These can be summarised as follows:

(1) Transition through regulation, based on public consensus (e.g. Sanne, 2002; Jackson, 2006);
(2) Radical transition through niche accumulation and system collapse (e.g. Trainer, 2014), or;
(3) Transition through a reconfiguration phase of consuming fewer, higher-quality products and services, combined with a subsequent and gradual culture change.

It is argued here that option one, while promising, is only feasible to a limited extent and only in certain social and political environments. Option two presents the most radical approach, but it excludes mainstream consumers, leaving them at the mercy of a system collapse at some point in the future. It is therefore proposed that – following Geels et al. (2015) – a third option is introduced, involving a continuation of consumer culture, but at a much-reduced level, through a shift from consuming quantity to consuming quality, i.e. the consumption of fewer items and services of higher quality and greater durability, while at the same time introducing the culture change needed to enable a genuine transition to sustainable consumption.

It would no doubt be preferable to move beyond the consumption de Graaf et al. (2001) have characterised as an epidemic of 'affluenza', which needs to be wiped out. We could further add that, as consumerism is a recent phenomenon, it should be reversible in some form. However, while the most popular tactics such as Hamilton's (2003) notion that we simply curb growth full stop in the expectation that people will automatically become happier might be appealing from an environmentalist standpoint, there is little to suggest that they would receive widespread popular support. A cynical audience unwilling to jeopardise the lifestyle they feel they are entitled to is likely to see this approach as utopian at best, at worst extremist on the conscious level. Subconsciously, many would probably feel an absence as this important means of building identity had been taken away, leaving them incomplete and thus possibly more predisposed to further mass consumption to try and fill the hole. Thus, we offer our idea of less but better consumption – allowing consumerist dreams of status and the construction of self through products to remain but in a more focused way that encourages quality over quantity. In addition, we have attempted to show how marketing could play a crucial role in this process.

There would be added benefits to be found if the desired objects of consumption were of themselves more sustainable – not just more durable, but, for example, less energy intensive – but this aspect should not necessarily be forced on consumers as that would defeat the point of managing consumption through tasking people with targeting their purchase habits to wants they most crave. It may well happen that, over time, changing attitudes and/or fashions may mean that, for example, the zero-emissions electric car takes on a higher social cachet than the gas-guzzling SUV in certain groups – as is increasingly the case for a subsection of liberal-minded celebrities for whom it is important to conceive of themselves and be seen by others as environmentally minded and virtuous (Newman, 2014). Further, it is important to consider, though, that even sustainable consumption of ethical goods (e.g. Fair Trade) can be seen to result in some manner of commodity fetishism whereby objects of consumption are given subjectivity beyond mere usage value (Carrier, 2010). As such, even the most enlightened consumer can struggle to move beyond the present age of consumption, meaning that our suggestion for less but better must be taken seriously as a means to promote the most sustainable patterns of consumption feasible for the present times.

PART II

Unsustainable production

8. Economies of scale and the roots of mass production

8.1   INTRODUCTION AND BACKGROUND

In Part II of this book, we investigate the production aspects of SCP. Mass consumption, or over-consumption, has only been made possible by mass production, which – as we will show – almost inevitably leads to over-production. As Sabel and Zeitlin (1985, 1997) have argued, mass production was never an inevitable outcome of historical developments in the late nineteenth and early twentieth centuries; it was the result of specific choices made at the time. Mass production largely came about because the US was rapidly expanding westwards as native American lands were expropriated and subjected to European economic methods and processes. This development required a lot of tools and, increasingly, machinery to cope with the scale of the project. Skilled craftsmen could usually find a secure living back in Europe, so were less likely to emigrate to the New World, which left a shortage of the skill-base needed to cater for this rapidly expanding market for new technology, tools and machinery. Thus, increasing automation to keep up with the sheer scale of demand was a natural choice. In this they could build on developments back in Europe resulting from the Industrial Revolution. In addition, the precision needed for certain products – notably firearms – combined with this lack of skilled craftsmen lent themselves well to automation. This was really the basis for the origin and growth of mass production in America. Similarly, in the garment industry, people could build on earlier developments in Europe, but – again – the sheer scale of demand from the expanding US empire ensured more than enough demand for an industry working at greater scale, where the lack of skilled weavers and seamstresses would be an added incentive. Other sectors, such as meat processing, focused on Chicago, and agriculture, had similar issues.

This at least explains why mass production became so prominent in the US. However, for understanding mass production in the context of SCP, the best example is the iconic one of mass car production, for reasons that will become clear. In brief, the mass production of cars, consisting of the various innovations in process introduced by Ford and symbolised by its moving production line, combined with the all-steel body technology, pioneered around the same time – the period around 1912–1914 – by Edward G. Budd and Joseph Ledwinka, not only transformed car production in the US, but also in Europe – where France was the first country to adopt it – and, ultimately, worldwide. In the process, the traditional craft producers, using hand-built engines and coach-building techniques for bodies on separate chassis frames were gradually but steadily marginalised and eventually largely squeezed out of the industry. In the US this happened in the 1930s, as analysed by Raff (1991, 1994), but in Europe this process extended into the 1950s.

Mass car production today is dominated by large centralised assembly facilities sourcing from worldwide networks of suppliers. The products of these large plants are dispatched to buyers worldwide via complex distribution networks largely featuring private dealerships not owned by the car manufacturers. Most of the key figures in the industry would – with Chandler (1977, 1990) – assume this is the final state of the automotive industry. This view of history is challenged by Lamoreaux et al. (2002), by Nieuwenhuis and Wells (2003, 2007, 2009) and also by Wynn-Williams (2009). However, it is clear that the present structure is closely linked with the adoption, by much of the car industry, of three interlocking strands of activity, for in addition to the technological contributions by Ford and Budd mentioned above, there was also the crucial contribution by General Motors under Sloan that made a mass car market possible by essentially creating demand for cars. Those contributions of Ford and Sloan (General Motors) have been well documented, both in a positive (Flink, 1988) and negative context (e.g. Freund and Martin, 1993). The third strand is Budd's all-steel body technology, the spread of which, in the interwar and immediate post-Second World War periods, has enjoyed significantly less attention, with analysis of this contribution being quite recent (Nieuwenhuis and Wells, 2007; Wynn-Williams, 2009). Figure 9.1 in Chapter 9 attempts to capture these three strands.

8.2 PREHISTORY: ORIGINS OF THE AUTOMOBILE

In 1885, and within about 100 km of each other, Carl Benz and Gottlieb Daimler each put an internal combustion engine in a vehicle and thereby initiated automobility and launched the car on its present trajectory. During the previous century a number of technologies had converged to allow the development of the internal combustion-engined car. These technological innovations were:

(1)   fast-running internal combustion engines;
(2)   bicycles, combining chain drive and a frame of steel tubes (the ability to make and bend tubes became crucial) and improved tyres;
(3)   developments in horse-drawn vehicles in terms of chassis and body, suspension, etc.

The fact that we regard the innovations by Benz and Daimler as embodying the technologies of the first car is an important point, because it highlights how we now see the car as primarily petrol-driven, despite the fact that steam-powered vehicles had been around since the late eighteenth century, while early battery-electric vehicles had been pioneered in the 1840s. Yet, it is only with the emergence of the petrol-driven car that we traditionally mark the birth of the motorcar. More broadly, this period saw the adoption of two new power sources in society generally: petroleum and electricity, continuing a process of moving to more and more concentrated sources of energy over time (Huber and Mills, 2005). In the new automotive sector, however, the new petrol engines had to compete with both established steam technology as well as the newly emerging use of electric power for machines. The development of fast-running industrial engines, suitable for powering petrol-powered vehicles, was the work of a few people, notably Otto in Germany, and the Belgian Lenoir. Soon after, Diesel, based in Germany like Daimler and Benz, though born in France, developed the compression-ignition engine, although its popularity had to wait a few more decades. The higher speeds of powered vehicles soon prompted improvements in suspension and steering, as well as tyres, the latter notably by Dunlop in the UK and by Michelin in France, who developed the pneumatic tyre, and the removable pneumatic tyre, respectively (Lottman, 2003).

Cars started life as craft-made products in that they were made one-by-one by hand with each being essentially different in detail and each component being different as it was adapted to its neighbours in the subassembly. Very rapidly, major suppliers were set up, particularly in France, able to supply engines, gearboxes, axles and other key components, allowing standardisation, a key precursor to mass production (Jeal, 2012). Jeal (2012) explains that standardisation did in fact exist in

Europe before Cadillac, Ford and others expanded on it in the US. Such standardisation was essential to allowing the production of the proprietary components that enabled the proliferation of early car-makers with very low levels of vertical integration. This process of standardisation in Europe was in fact the primary enabler for this proliferation of the number of brands between about 1895 and 1905. The key building blocks of cars were now available to all. Many firms assembled cars from bought-in components and limited themselves to fitting their own badge, itself often an outsourced part. The modular construction of cars at this time made this possible. Cars were almost invariably built up on a separate chassis frame, which carried all the components and subassemblies needed to make it move: engine, transmission, axles and wheels. This modular product is what Ford made at Highland Park, Michigan, the factory designed to build the iconic Model T (Nieuwenhuis and Wells, 1997, 2003, 2007). The body was a separate product and many car manufacturers sold their products as running chassis only. The owner would buy a body from a specialist coachbuilder, sometimes replacing it with a more modern one over time; a practice popular with the British royal family, for example (Smith, 1980). The car was thus often conceived of as consisting of its mechanical components; a running chassis, without the body.

8.3   FORD, BUDD AND SLOAN: THE HISTORY OF MASS CAR PRODUCTION

Nieuwenhuis and Wells (2007) sought the origins of mass car production in the combined technological and organisational innovations introduced by Ford and, especially the significant contribution made by Budd. However, in order to appreciate the overwhelming impact of these innovations on mass car manufacturing globally, it is important to understand the next phase by which Ford–Budd-style mass car production became the dominant paradigm to the virtual exclusion of any other car-making methods.

The role of Ford in the history of mass production has become contested, partly as a result of this earlier work (Nieuwenhuis and Wells, 1997, 2003, 2007; Nieuwenhuis, 2014). In order to substantiate this analysis, it has to be understood that mass car production today is very different from the way the Ford Model T was built at Highland Park, Michigan. Ford's Highland Park facility often made kits of parts that were then sent to various near-market Ford facilities to be assembled locally and fitted with local bodies. This happened in various locations in the US, but also abroad in places such as Trafford Park in Manchester, various locations in Australia, or Cork in Ireland. In fact, it was Ford's intention to move to a more decentralised car assembly model, far removed from the central-ised model that he and others subsequently developed, such as at River Rouge. As Ford put it:

> When we began to make our own parts we practically took for granted that they all had to be made in the one factory – that there was some special virtue in having a single roof over the manufacture of the entire car. We have now developed away from this. If we build any more large factories, it will be only because the making of a single part must be in such tremendous volume as to require a large unit ... This is a development which holds exceptional consequences, for it means ... that highly standardized, highly subdivided industry need no longer become concentrated in large plants with all the inconveniences of transportation and housing that hamper large plants. A thousand or five hundred men ought to be enough in a single factory ... (Ford, 1924: 84)

By contrast, mass car-making today is dominated by large, centralised assembly facilities sourcing from worldwide networks of suppliers. The products of these large plants are dispatched in fully finished form to buyers worldwide via complex distribution networks largely featuring private dealerships (see also Chapter 15). However, the main difference is that a modern car factory is centred around the production of body shells.

The notion that Ford was the first to mass produce cars is widely accepted. However, the car he mass produced, the Model T, was very much of its period, based on a modular approach to car-making as used by the previous generation of craft builders: separate chassis and separate, wood-framed, coach-built, or 'composite' body. This contrasts sharply with modern mass produced cars, and the distinctions here are crucial; today cars use all-steel 'monocoque', 'unit' or 'unibody' con-struction, whereby a structural welded metal box or bodyshell fulfils all structural functions. In other words, it acts as both body and chassis. This technology was made possible by the development, by Edward Budd and his chief engineer Joe Ledwinka, of the all-steel welded body in Philadelphia between about 1910 and 1914, i.e at about the same time that Ford introduced the moving assembly line (Nieuwenhuis and Wells, 1997, 2007). Thus Nieuwenhuis and Wells (2007) argue that modern mass car manufacturing owes at least as much to Budd and Ledwinka as it does to Henry Ford.

Modern, Budd-type steel body technology involves considerable capital investments in press, press tooling, welding and painting technologies, but once these investments are made, they allow for the low unit costs so typical of mass production. It is argued, therefore, that Budd's innovations constitute the very basis for the economics of the industry, notably in determining the crucial economies of scale in mass car production (Nieuwenhuis and Wells, 2003, 2007). This technological revolution involved the transition from the manufacture of modular cars from in-house components – typified by Ford's production system for the Model T at the Highland Park plant and later River Rouge in Dearborn, Michigan – to a situation where the manufacture of steel bodies formed the core activity. These were then assembled into cars from what today are largely outsourced components and subassemblies, but which Ford largely made in-house.

This system has been termed 'Buddism' (Nieuwenhuis and Wells, 2007) and it delivered well for the automotive industry while it was enjoying steadily expanding consumer demand, although in the more mature motorised countries a degree of market saturation set in from about the 1970s onwards. This led to a situation whereby market forces began undermining the Budd paradigm. Another development, emphasising the fact that this change is of a 'socio-technical' nature, is that this new technology proved eminently suited to successive increases in labour productivity via automation, to which the Budd system is particularly well suited. This affected all three of the main stages of production (press; weld; paint) hence offering continuous cost reduction and quality improvements, while also leading to a steady decline in the number of people employed in car making (Andera, 2007).

Today, markets expect much shorter product cycles, as well as more visible differentiation, leading to more diverse product ranges. These pressures mean lower volumes per model and thus a real danger of losing economies of scale. This is one of the primary reasons why profitability of mass car-making has shown a steady decline since its introduction in the 1920s. Attempts to recapture the economies of scale needed for profitable Budd-style car-making are one of the principal reasons for the industry's efforts to globalise and consolidate. Like the economic system of which it has become an integral part, the automotive mass production system requires constant growth in volume and newly motorising markets such as China, India or Brazil still allow large volumes of relatively standardised cars to be made and sold profitably thus extending the life of the traditional Ford–Budd mass production system. In fact, such markets – especially China – provide the foundation of much of the current profitability of firms like VW and GM and as a result provided much of the impetus for the economic recovery from the 2008 recession in Europe and North America.

9.   Importance of mass car production

But if mass car production was the result of conditions specific to North America, why did it spread globally? This is the focus of this chapter, with particular emphasis on how it became embedded in France, arguably the first country with what we could describe as a car industry. The term mass production 'paradigm' (Dosi, 1982) or 'regime' (Geels, 2002) could be used here because the system is not confined to the way cars are made, it determines also how they are sold, used and regulated to the extent that few observers today seem aware that this is not the only possible way to make and use cars. This is due to the fact that Budd-style car manufacturing has become closely integrated with the Fordist and Sloanist strands, as outlined in Figure 9.1, which also presents some of the factors that influenced each of these strands. This is in line with Rosenberg's notion (1979, 1982) that in order for automotive mass production to be realised it needed a series of complementary innovations, in this case the development of the all-steel body and the production processes needed to manufacture it, in parallel with those of Ford, as symbolised by the moving assembly line and innovations in the organisation of labour. In addition, this Fordist–Buddist system of mass supply needed a parallel system that promoted mass demand and it is this that constitutes Sloan's contribution. As argued by Tylecote and Vertova (2007), major innovations sometimes form clusters that combine to form technological systems with fundamental economic effects, a point also made by others (Tylecote, 1991; Freeman and Louçã, 2001). The three core elements of the mass car production system are a good example of this, although the additional, non-technological, socio-economic element of mass car markets and the resulting cultural and regulatory approaches should also be highlighted, making what some have described as a 'socio-technical regime' (e.g. Geels, 2002).

Figure 9.1, then, shows how the different strands of innovation came together to form this mass car production 'regime' or 'paradigm' and how it was built on a number of innovations that clustered together. These innovations included, for the Ford strand, the precision of interchangeable parts as exemplified by the light arms industry, and the moving pro-

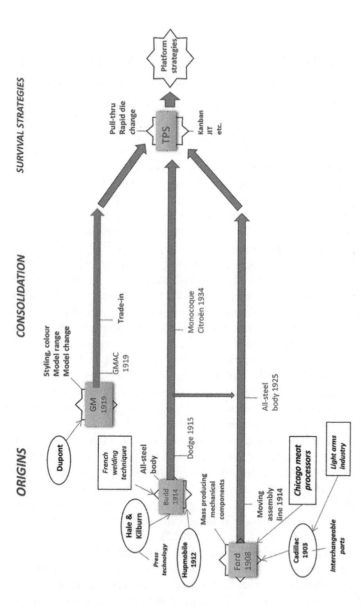

Figure 9.1   Key elements of mass car production

duction line, combined with discreet and simple production stages, as in meat processing in Chicago. The value of interchangeable parts was most famously demonstrated by Cadillac for the Dewar Trophy in 1908. For the Budd all-steel body strand (see Figure 9.2), we highlight the contribution of newly developed press and welding technologies, which Budd experienced at Hale and Kilburn in their railway carriage manufacturing business. The role of Hupmobile in commissioning an early pressed-steel welded body and subsequently the first major volume order for such bodies from Dodge Brothers are also significant milestones (see Figure 11.1). Also note that Ford did not adopt this technology until 1925 when production was transferred to the Rouge, while the further innovation of the all-steel unitary body or 'monocoque' was first used by Citroën, as set out below. The third strand, then, involves the various 'soft' innovations by GM under Sloan that promoted a car *market*. The final phase shows how Toyota was able to revitalise the system by a closer integration of these three strands, followed by others – notably Fiat, Honda and VAG (Nieuwenhuis and Wells, 1997) – who introduced the platform strategies that have allowed economies of scale to be retained while offering apparent diversity in the market.

The Fordist–Buddist technological manufacturing complex was inserted into an environment where, despite minor market fluctuations, on the whole demand outstripped supply; something further secured by the GM approach. It became therefore primarily supply-led with limited concern for any potential demand constraints. This is the context within which the 'origins' phase of Figure 9.1 plays out. Yet Freund and Martin (1993) argue that by the late 1920s, the US car market began to approach saturation, and they refer to contemporary market research in support of this view, which – they explain – showed that by 1926 those who could afford to own a car already owned one. Demand beyond this point, it is further argued, was therefore to a significant extent created by the active marketing of automobiles, notably at this time through the efforts of those adopting the Sloanite model pioneered by GM, but also rapidly adopted by, for example, Chrysler, which developed during this interwar era into the third major car-maker in the US. The key innovations contributed by GM during this period include large-scale vehicle finance through the creation of the General Motors Acceptance Corporation (GMAC) in 1919, the introduction during the 1920s of the trade-in, allowing an older car to be used in part payment for a new car, and, quite separately, the promotion of a dealer-supported used-car market. In addition, General Motors began to sell cars on style and colour rather than technology.

Figure 9.2   Budd all-steel body advertisement

This was made possible by a combination of Budd-style steel body technology – in the GM case supplied by Fisher – allowing new, more appealing shapes to be pressed in steel, and Dupont's newly developed paint processes (General Motors, undated (1926?), 1965). Dupont's part ownership of GM at this time was a crucial factor. The final key innovation within the Sloan armoury was the introduction of a product range, whereby customers could progress from entry-brand Chevrolet, via Oakland (later Pontiac), Buick and Oldsmobile, to La Salle and Cadillac; a system that was soon mirrored by Chrysler's product range where buyers were encouraged to progress from Plymouth to Dodge and on to Chrysler and Imperial. Once established, this system was enhanced with the notorious annual model change, which made cars a fashion object by creating the concept of 'planned obsolescence', in that a car became old not through age, but through being replaced by a model that was different, though not necessarily better; something abhorred by Henry Ford (Ford, 1924).

These innovations prompted buyers to think of the car no longer as a single item bought for life, as Henry Ford had intended (Ford, 1924: 149), but as a product that needed regular updating and replacement, ideally for a more upmarket model or brand. GM and Sloan are therefore crucial in this second, 'consolidation', phase highlighted in Figure 9.1. These innovations, and their manipulation of the market, allowed the supply-driven Ford–Budd manufacturing technologies at the heart of mass production to become firmly rooted over subsequent decades and for the economies of scale those technologies established to remain viable for many years. It is in this second phase that the French cases presented in Chapter 12 are situated. As mentioned, more recently, strategies can be observed that have thus far allowed the system to survive the vagaries of saturated markets demanding increasing differentiation. These strategies, the third phase outlined in Figure 9.1, include the tapping of new markets, notably China, India, Indonesia and Brazil, the development of the Toyota Production System, also known as 'lean production', and 'platform strategies' that allow high investment subassemblies, or 'architectures' in the Budd system to be shared among more model ranges thus protecting economies of scale in this highly capital-intensive part of the automotive value chain.

In technology terms, then, the key elements of modern car manufacturing centre on the mass production of the all-steel body and the internal combustion engine, contributed by Budd and Ford respectively. These innovations combined with those of Sloan have – as a growing number of suppliers developed able to take on the provision of components and subassemblies – shifted the centre of gravity of automotive firms' activities along different sections of the automotive value chain, such that the section of the value chain captured by Ford at Highland Park is different from that captured by General Motors under Sloan and different again from a modern mass producer. However, engines and steel bodies remain as core technologies under the control of all mass car manufacturers.

The Budd-inspired revolution in car manufacturing technology is a typical example of labour being replaced with capital and the subsequent trajectory of the car industry has seen a steady reduction in labour and an increase in capital per unit (cf. Andera, 2007). Although this has been partly made possible by the introduction of Budd-style all-steel body technology – in line with the 'labour-saving bias' (Blaug, 1963) – this was not its primary purpose. It is unlikely that the key players such as Budd or the Dodge Brothers foresaw the longer-term implications of their short- to medium-term business decisions, as David (1975: 4) has pointed out:

> … short-sighted choices about what to produce, and especially about how to produce it using presently known methods, also in effect govern what subsequently comes to be learned … may be far more important historically than the rational, forward-looking responses of optimizing inventors and innovators …

As a result of this type of path dependence, the automotive mass production and consumption system today is thus in line with Rosenberg's notion, the outcome of a series of not always obviously related processes and innovations that have, over time, become interlinked and have come to define what a mass car producer does (Rosenberg, 1979, 1982). It is also clear that, in the wake of Sloan's innovations, over time the emphasis of these activities has moved further down the value chain to capture more post-production, or 'after-sale' activities. In the process, some activities further up the supply chain – and perceived as being within the remit of a mass car producer a century ago – have been discarded or passed on to suppliers. This includes raw materials supply (Ford mined iron ore, owned rubber plantations, engaged in forestry), logistics, and the supply of between 60 and 80 per cent by value of the components that make up a car. Thus the core competence of the firm has shifted to encompass primarily brand management, systems integration, and, in technology terms, the internal combustion engine and the steel body. As

Sabel and Zeitlin (1985, 1997) have argued, mass production was but one of a range of manufacturing strategies, each of which was in reality of comparable technological validity. It is important to understand that Rosenberg's notion of complementary technologies being needed to make mass production possible was in this case achieved through a combination of chance and design. In this context, it is the second phase in Figure 9.1, and particularly the central process there, of embedding the Buddist technology model within the mass production system, which requires further explanation.

10. Origins of mass production: summary

Most observers accept the traditional notion that Ford was the first to mass produce cars and certainly the mass production of internal combustion engines can be attributed to his efforts. However, as Nieuwenhuis and Wells (2007) argue, the car he mass produced, the Model T, was an 'Edwardian' car, based on a modular approach to car-making: separate chassis and separate, wood-framed, or 'composite' body. Ford took the car as it was understood in his day, added some incremental improvements (Duncan, 2008; Casey, 2008) and adapted it to be mass produced. Modern mass-produced cars are not made like this. They use all-steel 'monocoque', or 'unibody' construction, whereby a welded, structural metal 'shell' fulfils the functions of both body and chassis. This technology was made possible by Budd and Ledwinka's invention of both the all-steel welded body and the press and jig technology that came with it. The all-steel body patent application was filed on 17 June 1914 under serial number 845,621and granted on 22 June 1914 in the name of Joseph Ledwinka (Budd, 1940). Edward Budd and Ledwinka, his chief engineer, took a systematic approach to converting the industry to all-steel bodies (Grayson, 1978; Courtenay, 1987). They also insisted on welding their bodies; the source of many development problems, but also of their claim to have started car-making on its current trajectory. Thus modern mass car manufacturing in many ways owes at least as much to Budd and Ledwinka as to Ford. While Fordism was possible without Budd, Toyotism refined Fordism within Budd technology in part by enhancing its responsiveness to market demand, the 'pull-through' concept. Yet, core Toyotist innovations such as rapid die changing are irrelevant without Budd and owe little to Ford. It is therefore surprising that the Toyotist literature (e.g. Womack et al., 1990) makes no mention of Budd.

Like Ford's mass production of mechanical components – notably engines – Budd's steel body technology requires very high initial investments, but once made, these allow low unit costs at high production volumes. Budd's innovations constitute the basis for the economics of

Table 10.1   Typical investments in a modern car assembly plant

Process	Typical cost (Euro)
Press shop	200 million
Die sets per model/variant	40–130 million
Body-in-white	100–200 million
Paint	400–600 million
Pre-assembly	20–100 million
Trim and final assembly	20–100 million
TOTAL	780–1330 million
Of which Budd all steel-related	740–1130 million

Source: Updated from Nieuwenhuis and Wells (2007).

car-making, notably its economies of scale (Nieuwenhuis and Wells, 2007; Wynn-Williams, 2009; Orsato, 2009). Table 10.1 shows the different areas of investment in a typical modern car plant, in which the first four rows represent investment in all-steel body technology. Engine production would add another €500–800 million, so it is clear that engine and body production are the largest investments by a considerable margin, with body technology investments combined slightly exceeding engine investments. This is partly due to the fact that while engines can be used across a number of model ranges, bodies need to be visibly distinct in order to create meaningful differentiation between models in the market. The main change, then, was from the manufacture of modular cars from largely in-house components at Ford's Highland Park plant, to the manufacture of steel bodies, assembled into cars from largely outsourced components and subassemblies in a typical modern mass production car plant. The in-house manufacture of engines and gearboxes – though not universal (BMW for example makes no gearboxes, while few manufacturers make automatic transmissions and with increasingly sophisticated transmission technology being adopted, this is increasingly outsourced) tends to be common to both. The next chapter investigates how this technology spread beyond the US, while evolving further into the modern automotive form, thereby lending further support to the historical basis for this 'Buddist' contribution to the mass car-making paradigm.

11. Europe takes the technology lead: the case of Citroën

Outside the US, the first car manufacturer to recognise the potential of Budd's new body technology was André Citroën, who went on a fact-finding tour of the US shortly after the First World War with a view to converting his wartime ammunitions facility to mass car production. Citroën visited both Henry Ford and Edward Budd and his firm was the first in Europe to adopt Dupont's quick-drying cellulose paints in 1924, soon after General Motors itself (Loubet, 2001). All-steel body technology is a logical next step as the ability to bake the paint speeds up the drying process even further. Budd technology allowed a steel body to be bake-enamelled and thus completed in a single day, whereas traditional 'composite' bodies would spend at least ten days in the paint shop (Budd, 1925). Thus, that same year, Citroën bought all-steel body technology from Budd in Philadelphia. Loubet explains that even in the US it was still rare due to its very high cost (Reynolds, 1996; Loubet, 2001). We must assume that this refers to the initial capital investment, rather than the unit cost per body, provided these are produced in sufficient numbers. In an industry still dominated by a myriad of smaller manufacturers, such a commitment to high volume would have been regarded as a deterrent – the ability to 'think big' was a first requirement. Also, being the first in Europe, Citroën could not benefit from Budd's own facilities, nor was the French firm apparently willing to take this route, preferring instead to bring as many processes as possible in-house (Loubet, 2001). It is also perhaps appropriate that a French manufacturer should be among the first to appreciate Budd and Ledwinka's innovation, as the Budd Co. relied heavily on French acetylene welding technology to develop its all-steel technology (Courtenay, 1987).

Citroën's interest in all-steel technology was prompted by the fact that the French firm ran into problems similar to those of Ford in that once mass production of mechanical components had been established, it was found that body construction and painting presented a major bottleneck preventing Citroën from moving to true mass production of complete cars (Loubet, 2001; Nieuwenhuis and Wells, 2003, 2007). Unlike Ford, Citroën shared Budd's longer-term vision and could see that the high costs of maintaining forests (or at least access to forestry products), large stocks of timber, sawmills and the highly skilled craftsmen needed to operate the ash-frame body system were unsustainable and could be avoided. In fact, even in the US, by the 1920s concern was being expressed about the depletion of forestry resources for car body manufacture and the use of alternatives was being promoted (Budd, 1925). Citroën also realised that without abandoning the wood-frame body, mass production was not possible.

By late 1924, the French firm had installed 156 new presses rated at 2,000 tonnes each, as well as 800 other machine tools for Budd all-steel body construction in a new factory at Saint-Ouen (Reynolds, 1996). When asked about the cost of this process, Citroën explained that 'One advances faster by taking giant steps, rather than small shuffles' (Reynolds, 1996: 66). Daily production in his plant rose from between 30 and 50 a day to between 400 and 500 a day, while production times were cut in half (Schweitzer, 1982). By 1925 nearly one in three cars in use in France were Citroën products – yet the firm only started making cars in 1919 (Reynolds, 1996). By 1926 the cost per body had dropped by FF1,000 (Loubet, 2001). Citroën production was up to 250 body sides and 200 chassis per hour and the company envisaged reducing its labour force from 14,000 to 10,000 for a production rate of 250 cars a day, while it was calculated that production levels of 500 cars a day could be reached with only 15,000 people (Loubet, 2001).

However, Citroën did become very reliant on US technology. All its major innovations in production, such as the all-steel body introduced in 1924; monocoque construction adopted in 1932 (though not entering production until 1934); power-assisted brakes introduced in 1924; and 'floating' engine mountings introduced in 1932 – the need for which is a by-product of Budd technology – relied on US technology and patents. In addition to royalty payments on each car sold (Budd received between $1 and $3 on each body made: Loubet, 2001: 105), Citroën had to invest some $600,000 in the monocoque system for the Traction Avant model (Loubet, 2001; and see below). The cost of this body technology was very high in terms of investment in machinery, as well as the need to source from the US the higher grades of steel needed to make it work (Loubet, 2001). In 1926, these special steels cost FF4.5 per kilogramme, rather than the FF2.6 of standard French automotive steel. Each Budd car body used 500 to 600 kg of steel sheet. Although André Citroën had declared

in 1923 that 'Dès l'instant où une idée est bonne, le prix n'a pas d'importance' (from the moment an idea is good, price becomes unimportant),
the cost of Budd technology must now be regarded as a major contrib-
utor to Citroën's bankruptcy in 1934 (Reynolds, 1996). In this context,
Tylecote and Vertova's (2007) assertion that cheap steel was essential to
mass car production is therefore pertinent; Citroën was engaged in a constant battle to reduce the cost of steel per car. Setting up its own steel mill
in Froncles saved FF1,000 per car; 10 per cent of the cost of materials
(Loubet, 2001). Nonetheless, Citroën still had to import pressings from
Budd in the US. In 1927, this amounted to 20,000 pressings at a total
cost of $500,000, to allow a rapid introduction of the crucial B14 model.
The French firm even set up a new purchasing office in Detroit for this
purpose. It was found that with the rapidly rising production volumes
noted above, French suppliers could not keep up with the numbers of
parts needed – a problem Ford had encountered some 20 years earlier –
nor could they supply at the same cost as US firms. Ultimately Citroën set
up much of this capability back in France, although the FF8 million spent
on steering and clutch production saved only FF200 per car, 1 per cent of
the ex-factory price (Loubet, 2001).

11.1 CITROËN AND MONOCOQUE CONSTRUCTION: BUDD'S IMPACT ON CAR DESIGN

The history of the monocoque or unibody is initially to some extent a separate narrative from the all-steel body in that the first Budd applications
still used a separate body and chassis; a practice that persisted in some
firms longer than in others, particularly in North America (Mac New,
1955; Weinert, 1957; Nieuwenhuis and Wells, 1997, 2007). However,
Budd pressed steel technology certainly made this the obvious next
step in vehicle construction. Budd found that by using single body-side
stampings, some of the load on the chassis could be fed into the body,
thus allowing an overall weight reduction for chassis and body combined
(Thum, 1928). This is the technology stage that made the innovative and
influential Chrysler Airflow design possible, for example. In 1934 it was
Chrysler brand De Soto that introduced partial unitary body construction
on the landmark Airflow Series SE, while Chrysler member firm Dodge
was the first major producer to adopt Budd all-steel bodies from 1915
onwards, albeit before it was part of Chrysler (Courtenay, 1987; Vellicky
and Pitrone, 1992; Hyde, 2005). In 1923 it launched, with Budd, the

all-steel Series 116-FOUR which was the first Dodge all-steel closed body (the body advertised in Figure 11.1 still used a fabric upper body). It also pioneered the baked-enamel finish to replace its traditional paint/ varnish system. This was all made possible by the use of Budd all-steel technology. However, the Airflow design was as far as any US firm was prepared to take Budd technology towards full unibody construction at that time.

The Budd Company itself did conduct some early experiments with steel monocoques (Courtenay, 1987; Taylor, 1994) and Ledwinka filed a patent application for a steel unibody as early as 1927 (Grayson, 1978). However, in terms of production vehicles, it was the Europeans who took this next step, albeit with Budd input (Taylor, 1994). Early examples of all-steel monocoque or unibody construction are the Citroën 11CV/15CV or 'Traction Avant' of 1934 and built until 1956, and the 1935 GM Opel Olympia. The latter's derivative, the 1938 Opel Kadett, was later made in the Soviet Union as a Moskvitch, further committing the Soviets to the Buddist manufacturing introduced with the ZIS 101 (Automotive Industries, 1935a, 1935b; Eckermann, 1989; Besch, 2002). Edward Budd himself also saw the monocoque as the logical next step in steel body development (Motor, 1937). However, Budd also saw some disadvantages; among them the need for greater accuracy as well as the problem of assembling the car after the unibody has been built, which requires greater care on the part of assembly workers to avoid damage to the painted body. This is indeed still an issue in modern car assembly, which is generally addressed by means of protective covers on the painted body during assembly and removal of the doors after painting. The latter is a procedure pioneered by the Japanese, but it needs very thorough production sequencing to ensure that the correct doors are reunited with the correct body. This seemingly trivial process itself has forced considerable improvements in manufacturing logistics on all firms that have introduced this by now virtually universal process. Budd was doubtful, however, if there was a cost advantage to unibody construction (Motor, 1937).

It is possible that this line of thinking is behind the retention of some sort of vestigial chassis on many full-size US cars until the late twentieth century – and many SUVs into the early twenty-first century; thus Budd spent much of its history still welding steel chassis (Mac New, 1955; Weinert, 1957). On the other hand, Taylor (1994) suggests that Citroën believed there could be a cost advantage, while Budd did expect a slight weight advantage and described the move as a radical innovation, which

Source: The Saturday Evening Post, 4 November 1922, p. 43.

Figure 11.1   Dodge Brothers advertisement

indeed it turned out to be, changing mass car production for a long time to come. Weight reduction was already more relevant in Europe than in the US at this time. One major difference between automobility in the US and Europe had already arisen. The US with its own oil supplies was still self-sufficient in automotive fuel, allowing a low fuel cost and low energy-efficiency culture to become established among its car designers, builders and customers. Although some European countries had limited oil reserves, even with low levels of motorisation none were self-sufficient in terms of vehicle fuels. The larger oil reserves found in the North Sea in the 1960s and 1970s came at a time when a more frugal automotive culture was well established and in any case with the prevailing levels of motorisation in the 1970s, 1980s and 1990s, UK supplies were depleted within a few decades, with only Norway, with its much smaller population, retaining significant reserves. Weight reduction as a means of achieving greater fuel efficiency was already a significant design criterion in Europe as early as the 1930s; it was thus a major design motivation, which the Americans lacked. There was also a financial incentive to reduce weight and thus material use.

The weight advantage of monocoque construction was confirmed by the 1935 Opel Olympia, which weighed some 110 kg less than its otherwise equivalent predecessor – a saving of 11 per cent in vehicle weight (Eckermann, 1989). Citroën was also hoping to reduce vehicle weight by 100 kg by adopting this technology (Loubet, 2001). The concept of this car – the 1934 Traction Avant – was ultimately supplied by a new recruit, rejected by Renault, but highly recommended by his former employer, the aircraft and car manufacturer Gabriel Voisin, who had always advocated weight reduction (Taylor, 1994; Berk, 2009). Voisin achieved weight reduction for his sporty luxury cars through extensive use of aluminium and very simple body structures without 'useless adornment' and later also without wood (Bellu, 1988; Courteault, 1991; Berk, 2009). André Levebvre had used his experience at Voisin – which introduced monocoque racing cars as early as 1923 (Lefebvre was in fact one of its racing drivers, as well as playing a major role in designing the car) – to develop a radical new car concept which involved front wheel drive, torsion bar suspension, hydraulic brakes and monocoque construction for a total weight of no more than 750 kg (Loubet, 2001; Berk, 2009).

As mentioned above, Citroën paid $600,000 to instal the body system for its monocoque Traction Avant. This was offset by a saving of 70 kg in steel per car, which, in view of the high-cost steel needed, meant a financial saving of FF300–500 per car (Loubet, 2001). Although

Citroën was the first to produce a monocoque structure in volume production, it relied heavily on Budd's patents and technologies to do this, putting Budd employee Kendall in charge of production (Reynolds, 1996). In fact, even Flaminio Bertoni's styling of the car – with input from Jean Daninos who later founded the Facel body company which also ventured into car-making (see Section 12.2) – also closely followed Budd's monocoque prototype, which a team from Automobiles Citroën – which included André Citroën himself – had seen in Philadelphia in 1931 (Taylor, 1994). Budd's prototype also, significantly, had front wheel drive, a system still rare at that time on both sides of the Atlantic. Front wheel drive had been tried on some sports and racing cars (e.g. Tracta in France, Alvis in the UK), some specialist cars (e.g. Cord in the US from 1929) and a few mass-produced cars, notably in Germany by DKW (1932) and Adler for its Trumpf (1932).

The move to monocoque construction had a greater immediate impact than front wheel drive. For this reason its intellectual property was vigorously defended. Renault later copied the Opel Olympia/Kadett concept for the Juvaquattre and fell foul of Budd's patents and copyrights. In fact, Budd repeatedly threatened to sue Renault for infringement of patents and copyright before they finally paid compensation (Grayson, 1978). That Budd took its intellectual property seriously was also illustrated by the earlier case against the C. R. Wilson Body Co. (Automotive Industries, 1926). However, Renault personnel, on a fact-finding tour of the US after the liberation, did find that Europe had by then overtaken the Americans in exploiting the possibilities of Buddist car design. They took two prototype Renault 11CV models to Budd in 1945, which Budd – who developed the bodies – calculated would weigh around 1,100 kg. In fact, Renault succeeded in making them at 900 kg (Loubet, 2001). The Americans, meanwhile had focused more on styling and advances in production methods involving the implementation of both Fordist and Buddist ideas, as well as implementing much greater specialisation, such as plants making only a single model line, something European car-makers with their much lower volumes could rarely afford to do without achieving minimum economies of scale.

12. The death of craft production: Ford and Budd's impact on the French car industry

Although the car industry shifted to Budd technology, most of it eventually adopting monocoque construction, individual firms did not universally take this route. In the US, most small craft car-makers did not survive the 1930s (Raff, 1991, 1994). Raff does not include Budd specifically in his analysis but he points out that the Chevrolet division of General Motors was the first to adopt mass production after Ford, in the late 1920s. Around this time, Fisher all-steel technology made an impact at GM. However, Raff also explains that most of the US car industry remained craft-based, arguing that 'the key to Ford's production success was not understood by contemporaries' (Raff, 1991: 727). In fact, the effect of all-steel technology was even less well understood, in part because key works on the history of mass production often focused their analysis on periods too early for the full impact of this technology to have manifested itself. Even a more recent work, such as Hounshell (1984), chooses to cover developments only up to 1932 when the full impact of the technologies outlined here had not yet played out. It is clear, though, that the GM management did understand its significance, as illustrated by the fact that – as explained by Helper and Sako (2010) – one of the reasons for the takeover of Fisher Body was that it enabled them to put the Fisher brothers in charge of GM strategy; their understanding of increasingly core all-steel body technology now making them invaluable to GM.

Most US car-makers did not adopt mass production at all, as a result of which most went out of business. Raff argues that the diffusion of mass production happened primarily through the entry and exit of firms rather than through changes in the methods of existing firms (Raff, 1991). There is some truth in this, as Dodge Brothers, for example were a new entrant when they introduced the Budd system to the industry. However, others – including Ford (Nieuwenhuis and Wells, 2007) – adopted Budd technology, albeit relatively late in 1925 (Ford Motor

Co., 1929), while GM adopted all-steel technology within a couple of years after that through its Fisher Body division; Raff's statement therefore appears to be an overgeneralisation. Raff (1994) explains that by 1929, the Big 3 were responsible for about three-quarters of US car output; the remainder being made up of specialist quality cars, such as Pierce-Arrow, Auburn-Cord-Duesenberg, and others. These firms did manage to practice cost recovery and had significantly better margins than the mass producers. Raff explains that the reason they failed was that while the mass producers relied on capital assets they could dispose of during the Depression and subsequently replace, the specialists' assets were their skilled staff. Once made redundant, their skills were lost to the firm and quality and productivity suffered. Most recognised this and tried to retain staff, but the economic crisis lasted simply too long. However, ultimately it is unlikely they would have been able to compete without adopting mass-produced engine technology and, possibly all-steel body technology. A special case here is luxury producer Packard, which did adopt mass production technologies, including all-steel bodies, alongside its more conventional coach-built products, which in turn acted as 'halo' models to enable premium pricing on the more high-volume products (Turnquist, 1965; Foster, 2017). Packard was thus able to premium price what were in effect mass-produced cars, albeit complex ones; in this sense it pre-dates later examples such as BMW. However, the increasing struggle of traditional coach-built car-makers is further illustrated by the fate of their French counterparts, the makers of 'grandes routières', the French sporty luxury cars that were the choice of the fashionable world-wide during the 1930s; something that is explored next, to highlight the cost of change.

12.1   THE COST OF TRANSITION: DEMISE OF THE FRENCH LUXURY CAR INDUSTRY

Loubet (2001) describes how an American fact-finding tour in 1946 was astonished to see almost state-of-the-art mass production at Citroën and Renault, side by side with the anarchic craft production at luxury producer Delahaye. However they did conclude that the long cycle times at Renault and Peugeot pointed to 'a modern concept of mass production improperly applied' (Loubet, 2001: 229). They felt there was too much manual input in Peugeot's plant at Sochaux and Renault's at Billancourt, and flows that were too erratic (Loubet, 2001). This can probably be attributed to the generally lower volumes produced by European car firms, which have consistently challenged their ability to reach true economies of scale by comparison with their US counterparts. Also, at this point labour costs were considerably higher in the US than in France; here the case for replacing labour with capital was therefore less compelling. The point about the anarchic craft production is interesting as this sector had by then been wiped out in the US – as discussed earlier and as outlined by Raff (1994).

The effect of the 1929 Wall Street crash was significantly smaller in France compared with the US or UK, due in part to the persistence of small family businesses in France as well as traditionally high savings rates (Reynolds, 1996). Thus the French specialist car producers had not been hit to quite the same extent as the impact analysed by Raff for the US (1994). By the mid 1930s, France still boasted a number of specialist, low-volume producers of craft-built luxury cars, notably: Delage, Delahaye, Hispano-Suiza (which also had a Spanish branch), Talbot-Lago, Bugatti, Voisin, Hotchkiss and Salmson. Even so, at that point, some of these were in crisis and by the end of the decade several had gone. Voisin essentially stopped production in 1939 (Courteault, 1991), Hispano-Suiza abandoned car-making in favour of aircraft engine production in 1937 (Green, 1977; Badré, 1990), while Delage and Delahaye merged (Rousseau, 1978; Dorizon et al., 1995). All the survivors moved upmarket during the 1930s and found there were still enough wealthy people around for them to trade on lower volumes and higher margins. They all survived occupation in some form and by the late 1940s new models (often new body styles on pre-war chassis) were launched by Delage-Delahaye, Hotchkiss, Talbot-Lago, Salmson and even, tentatively, by Bugatti, although its 101 model was made in minute numbers (Conway, 1987). Some additional consolidation did take place as Hotchkiss took over Delage-Delahaye (Fouquet-Hatevilain, 1983, 1995), while mass producer Simca absorbed Talbot-Lago (Borgé and Viasnoff, 1981; Spitz, 1983). Salmson was primarily an aircraft engine producer and survives as an automotive supplier (Fouquet-Hatevilain, 1986). Some luxury manufacturers – Hotchkiss and Delahaye in particular – were also helped by military contracts after the war.

These firms used traditional craft-based methods with in-house production of mechanical components, notably engines, which they regarded as core technology. Running chassis were then dispatched to the customer's coachbuilder of choice for a bespoke body to be fitted. Over time, some standardisation began to set in with some offering bodies by in-house coachbuilders at lower cost, while consolidation in engines

Table 12.1   Car sales in France: selected companies and years

Company	Manufacturing technology	1939	1950	1955	1959
Citroën	Mass	54,240	38,434	106,163	158,815
Renault	Mass	33,462	55,080	125,439	169,119
Hotchkiss	Craft	1,935	1,350	140	1
Salmson	Craft	852	960	87	0
Talbot	Craft	531	290	13	6

Source: Adapted from Nieuwenhuis and Wells (1997: 198).

came with consolidation of firms – Delahaye-Delage eventually limited choice to the 3-litre straight-six Delahaye engine. However, other than Voisin on its swan-song model (based on an American Graham), none took the step of offering a mass-produced engine. Tables 12.1 and 12.2 illustrate how specialist, craft-built cars had become uncompetitive with modern mass-produced cars in the French market. By 1950 both types of construction still attempted to compete in several of the French fiscal horsepower segments defined by their 'chevaux vapeur' (CV). In the lower, 4CV segment the craft model carries a price premium of some 30 per cent, while in the 15CV segment the price premium is nearer 60 per cent. Only some of this could be compensated for through cost recovery – there is a limit to how much even wealthy buyers are prepared to pay for a prestige badge.

The marginal competitiveness of their products was illustrated by the fact that by the early 1950s the most exclusive car – Delahaye's 235 – had become ten times more expensive than the popular Citroën 2CV (Table 12.2). By contrast, in the pre-mass production days, French cars could be placed in three broad pricing bands ranging from around FF5,000 to above FF10,000 with the vast majority selling in the FF5,000–10,000 band (Laux, 1976). Loubet (2001) and Laux (1976) also illustrate that in terms of pricing and volume, there were no major differences before the First World War between what would later become volume and niche manufacturers (Table 12.3).

The difference in relative prices between the period before World War I, when all French manufacturers used craft-based methods with coach-built bodies, and the early 1950s, when some had adopted Ford–Budd style mass production is striking (Table 12.2) and must to a large extent reflect the differential production costs between mass and craft production. Despite lower investment levels in tooling (i.e. avoidance

Table 12.2   *Typical prices of French cars 1950–1955*

Make	Model	Production system	Price (FF)
Citroën	2CV	Mass	289,000
	11CV Traction Avant	Mass	558,700
	15-Six Traction Avant	Mass	754,800
Renault	4CV	Mass	430,000
Peugeot	203	Mass	577,000
Simca	Sport	Mass/coach-built body	1,400,000
Panhard	Dyna	Mass	569,000
Ford	Vedette	Mass	848,000
Salmson	G-72	Craft	1,480,000
Hotchkiss	Anjou	Craft	1,290,000
Talbot-Lago	Baby	Craft	1,300,700
Delahaye	235	Craft	2,800,000

Source: Compiled from data in Sabatès (1986).

of expensive press tools by the craft producers), other costs, notably labour, higher-cost low-volume purchasing, marketing and distribution took away any advantage this might have brought. The final battle came in the 1950s and was lost by the luxury craft car-makers. The enemy was formed by a combination of factors, notably: high taxation on luxury cars imposed by left-leaning governments in France, but perhaps more importantly, fierce competition from credible mass-produced French cars such as the Citroen 15-six and ID/DS, as well as imported luxury cars using mass-produced engines and all-steel technology. The import threat came particularly from Mercedes-Benz in Germany and Jaguar in the UK. Both firms were able to offer luxury cars at a fraction of the price of their French competitors. Although wealthy buyers might appreciate a unique coach-built body, few could see advantages in a hand-built engine over a mass-produced engine of similar performance.

Jaguar introduced monocoque construction with the 2.4 in 1956, which was still quite novel for a luxury car at the time (Montague of Beaulieu, 1975), but had introduced Budd-style all-steel technology shortly after the Second World War, while consolidating on a single six-cylinder engine design throughout its model range. With its origins in coach-building, Jaguar's William Lyons saw the advantages of all-steel construction for luxury cars, while war work provided the firm with an understanding of modern mass production practices it could apply to both engine and body

Table 12.3   _Price and volume comparison model ranges French manufacturers pre-WWI (production in units 1913; prices in FF)_

Manufacturer	Production 1913	10CV*	12CV	15/16CV	18CV	20CV	24/25CV	50CV	60/70CV
Darracq	3,500	7,000	12,000	0	0	15,000	17,500	25,000	0
De Dion	2,800	0	0	10,000	0	0	15,500	0	0
Panhard	2,100	0	0	12,000	14,500	0	20,000	32,000	0
Peugeot	5,000	5,000	7,500	10,300	13,500	14,000	18,500	24,000	28,000

Note: * Indicates model designation in power output (CV).
Source: Adapted from Laux (1976: 199) and Loubet (2001: 42).

Table 12.4   Coach-built versus Budd-style luxury car price/
            performance (France, 1961)

Make	Model	Body technology	Engine technology	Price (FF)	Power h.p.	Top speed kph
Aston Martin	DB4	Coach-built	Craft	65,000	243	225
Bentley	S 2	Coach-built	Craft	95,000	n/a	175
Buick	Electra	Budd	Mass	43,190	325	175
Chevrolet	Corvette	Fibreglass	Mass	45,000	250	180
Citroën	DS19	Budd	Mass	15,550	83	150
Facel Vega	Facel II	Budd	Mass	53,000	390	240
Jaguar	3.8 Mk II	Budd	Mass	31,000	223	200
Lancia	Flaminia	Semi-coach-built	Mass	34,000	140	200
Mercedes	300 SE	Budd	Mass	32,000	160	225

Source: Compiled from data in Pascal (1998: 27).

manufacturing. Lyons could see that by building luxury cars in volume he would be able to compete on price – even wealthy buyers appreciate value for money. In 1947, over £100,000 was spent on machine tools for mechanical components and body tooling, though body construction was subcontracted to Pressed Steel, an early Budd licensee (Montague of Beaulieu, 1975; Grayson, 1978; Harvey, 1981). Pressed Steel made complete Jaguar bodyshells using Budd technology; Jaguar thus benefited from the economies of scale its supplier achieved by making bodies for a range of manufacturers; a key part of the Budd model from the start. The cost of presses was shared with other clients, Jaguar only having to cover the cost of its own tooling. Budd technologies allowed much higher production volumes than were customary in the specialist car sector in Europe at the time – wood was used for trim, not body construction, at Jaguar. Jaguar built 9,660 cars in 1946–1948, a figure which was soon to become closer to annual production. This move to higher volumes allowed cost-effective mass production of its single engine type – the XK – and competitive pricing and Jaguar was consistently able to undercut more traditional competitors on price (Table 12.4).

    The effect of the introduction of Buddism and Fordism on the French car industry was significant. There was a rapid rise in the number of French car-makers from its beginnings in the 1880s. After an initial shake-out between 1900 and 1910, a period of stability set in. However the interwar period saw a major decline with the various economic crises and the introduction of mass production by some manufacturers, notably Citroën and Renault, taking its toll. The post-World War II period saw a slight revival as plastics technology made some new small-volume producers viable (Alpine, DB, Gordini, etc.) and an increase in demand allowed the luxury craft makers, such as Delahaye, Hotchkiss, Salmson and Talbot, a brief stay of execution. From 1950 the final decline set in, resulting in the present handful of car-makers in France: Renault, PSA Peugeot-Citroën, Mega and a handful of other small-scale producers. This effect was not limited to France. France has the world's oldest car industry and therefore illustrates such trends perhaps better than most other industries. However, the spread of Ford's mass production, supported by Budd-style body, technology gradually moved around the world.

12.2 THE CASE OF FACEL

The case of Facel is an interesting one. As a car manufacturer, this was a new start-up company entering the market in 1954. The founder, Daninos, had worked for Citroën, while he had also witnessed the gradual decline of craft-based French luxury producers and felt he had found a formula that would allow him to work around the limitations of craft production for high-end low-volume vehicles (Daninos, 1981). Forges et Ateliers de Construction d'Eure et Loir (Facel) Metallon became a firm experienced in sheet steel fabrication, particularly stainless steel (Sedgwick, 1973). From this activity it expanded to become an independent coach-building firm of a more modern type, using Budd all-steel technology to produce small runs of specialised bodies on mass-produced chassis, allowing mass producers to expand their product ranges at minimal cost, whilst being able to command a premium in the market. Daninos was aware of mass production techniques and particularly Budd technology from his days at Citroën (Daninos, 1984: 11; Renou, 1984). His solution for his own car, the Vega, was to offer standardised pressed-steel bodies fitted to an in-house chassis – thereby avoiding the more expensive and complex monocoque construction – and powered by a mass-produced Chrysler V8 engine. As with other surviving specialist manufacturers, such as Morgan in the UK, this formula of outsourcing engines from mass producers worked well (Nieuwenhuis and Katsifou, 2015). The smaller cost premium resulting from using Budd body technology for low-volume production could be offset by cost recovery from an exclusive brand. Where traditional luxury producers such as Delahaye and Hotchkiss had suffered the combined cost penalty of craft bodies and craft engines, Facel benefited from sharing Chrysler's economies of scale in engines, which he claimed to buy at an 'extremely interesting price' (Daninos, 1981: 23). An additional and significant advantage was that Facel made small-production-run bodies for other manufacturers, such as Panhard, Ford of France and Simca, as well as making Vespa scooter bodies for Piaggio, and was thus also able to share some of these facilities – such as a press shop at Amboise and paint shop at Colombes – for its own cars (Daninos, 1981; Renou, 1984; Demoulin, 2000). Effectively, his clients funded his economies of scale. Only the cost of die sets and product development were significant investments, although Facel Metallon also had the expertise to make its own die sets, so these costs were internalised to a large extent. Problems arose when Facel attempted to introduce a smaller model, the Facellia. No French producer was willing to supply engines for what they perceived as a competitor, so Daninos made the crucial error of developing his own engine, contracting his gearbox supplier, Pont-à-Mousson, to build the engines. Serious reliability problems ensued while a rapid re-engineering of the car and re-sourcing to Volvo engines came too late to save the brand image and avoid the very high warranty costs. Because of the small scale of Facel, these factors were crucial in causing the company's demise in 1964 (Sedgwick, 1973; Renou, 1984).

13. Mass production in food

Another example we would like to bring in is that of the food industry and how it has also become dominated by the mass production paradigm, especially in the West, and as such is highly unsustainable. Mass produced or industrialised food systems are interestingly often labelled as 'conventional' systems – as opposed to 'alternative' food systems which are discussed later in this section (Marsden et al., 2000; Sonnino and Marsden, 2006). Food is an interesting space to consider as humans will always need food to survive, yet what we are seeing nowadays is a deeply flawed production and consumption food system where food scarcity and poverty co-exist with over-production and over-consumption, which is in turn responsible for growing obesity and associated diseases. So how did we get to this?

There are many reasons and factors that have led and contributed to the advent of mass food production in the West and to making it seem a desirable paradigm worldwide. The rest of the discussion below is by no means exhaustive but sheds light on some of the interrelated aspects that have been conducive to mass food production. The rise of mass food production cannot be understood separately from the industrialisation of our economies. We do not only refer here to the possibilities that industrialised production offered in terms of food production, but rather to how it went hand-in-hand with the rise of a new working class. The narrative of work as it emerged and got shaped by the industrialisation and urbanisation of society is conceptualised around questions of freedom, autonomy and value-creation. Under the growth-obsessed capitalist economic paradigm, paid employment is the only type of work that is valued as it is constructed as the only form of productive work. This last point resonates with our discussion on growth in Chapter 5, Section 5.1. As labour outside the home became the *norm*, so valuable/valued, home-based work, including caring duties and the growing as well as preparation of food, increasingly became a constraint that required outsourcing. Interestingly, we can also see how such a path has linkages with movements such as the one for the emancipation of women, and in some way has certainly benefitted a large part of the population. With such processes of outsourcing and more time spent at work outside the home, we have witnessed an important loss of skills and knowledge around food in many households over generations, i.e. food growing and cooking, which has simply contributed to reinforcing the view that food production needs to be outsourced.

One cannot think of the developments above without considering the accompanying technologies that have emerged from and supported them. Some examples include the Chorleywood bread process, the development of ever-more resistant and high-yield crops and seeds that can be grown in many conditions, and the rise of the packaging and fertiliser industries, to name but a few. In addition, it is obvious that the trends described above mean that the industrialisation of food production goes hand in hand with the centralisation of food purchasing and mass food consumption. While supermarkets only emerged much later as the dominant form of food retail in the West, they have contributed to an acceleration of the mass food paradigm and especially of a normalisation of the idea of the constant availability of cheap food (Figure 13.1).

The paradigm of mass food consumption and production hence is constructed, legitimised and sustained through a paradoxical narrative of abundance (of cheap food at all times) versus scarcity (of time for individuals) within food systems. This has paved the way for the rise and domination of large food companies – from manufacturing and retailing, to restaurants – and of global food chains. What we see now are highly concentrated food systems, controlled and dominated by a handful of large players (McCarthy et al., 2018), from those that provide the inputs into agriculture (think Monsanto), through those that purchase agricultural goods (e.g. Nestle, Unilever ...), to retail of manufactured/transformed food products (e.g. supermarket giants like Tesco and Walmart). Over the last few decades, fast food chains have also proliferated, and are even seen as a sign of societal progress and freedom. They have blossomed in recent years in places like China and Iran, as desirable places to go and eat, indicating not only wealth but trendiness and open-mindedness. All these 'giant food corporations' (Tsing, 2009) rely on highly industrialised, fragmented and geographically dispersed supply chains. These global food chains are predicated upon and perpetuate deeply ingrained inequitable systems of production, whereby consumption in the Global North is served through the continued exploitation of natural resources and labour from the Global South (McCarthy et al., 2018).

The vast majority of consumers in the West have therefore become detached from their food and its provenance (McCarthy et al., 2020).

*Figure 13.1   Pre-sliced white bread has come to symbolise
mass-produced food*

They also want it cheap, available immediately and at all times.
Seasonality is a lost concept in most Western societies. The general
public's lack of understanding of natural cycles not only means a clear
disconnect with the rural world and the agriculture that are the sources
of food, it also has served the development of food technologies such as
greenhouses and irrigation to serve the year-round demand for products
such as tomatoes and strawberries. The advent of mass food consumption
and production has had positive effects in terms of food availability and
access, but these are increasingly seen as very limited. Mass-produced
food and the rise of branded food products have translated into the creation of food *wants*, particularly of manufactured ready-made meals and
complex food snacks, many with limited or no nutritional value. These
are often more easily available than fresh and healthy food products and

marketed as convenient and value for money, making them appealing choices. It is no surprise then that we have witnessed a rise in obesity rates across many Western countries. In addition, the persistence and growth of areas with limited access to healthy food – for which the term 'food deserts' has been coined (Wang et al., 2018) – are clear symptoms of the unsustainability of our food systems.

Lang (1999: 169) argues that 'food systems and supply chains are the product of policy and political choices ... characterised by large scale concentration and centralisation, both politically and economically'. Food and agriculture are indeed a key agenda for public policy and many governments across Europe and North America have so far nurtured the rhetoric of ever more available cheap food (otherwise they risk entering into the minefield of providing everyone with a decent income to afford food) and have promoted the advancement of technology. This provides an even stronger basis for more corporate control over food production. In recent years we have also seen a strong focus on the sustainability and future of food systems. Coupled with the narrative of 'feeding a growing population', this is an agenda which so far has been once again dominated by the large corporations and has embraced the technofix paradigm.

The future of food is up for debate, however, and it is unlikely that technology will be our salvation if we are to pursue a more ecologically sustainable and equitable path. For instance, much is written in terms of the environmental impact of agriculture, and particularly in relation to animals (i.e. dairy and meat production). The emphasis is often placed on minimising the footprint of these activities – with accompanying technology – rather than truly challenging the premise upon which our food systems are based, i.e. over-production to serve over-consumption. As such, the technology rhetoric is seen as more appealing than the fundamental rethinking of our food systems, and has also been embraced by many food scientists, who are proponents of *tech as salvation*. We see discussions of farming at gigantic scales, so-called 'fermes de mille vaches' (Valiorgue and Hollandts, 2019), to enable ever-more efficiency and control over natural processes. Once again, the human/nature distinction here is key to understanding this: we treat everything non-human as commodified objects. The models make additional promises of less environmental impact, but at what ethical cost? We also see proponents of food grown in the lab as the most sustainable future (e.g. Monbiot, 2020). These arguments, however, are often based upon flawed understandings of the energy provision requirements behind lab-grown food and of their socio-economic implications. There is a huge social cost in terms of how this would destroy farming and agriculture. In addition, it is deeply questionable to suppose that such modes of production could meet the collective interest of producing healthy and more sustainable food, given the power of big corporations, which would tend to control these laboratory processes. The potential for even further concentration and oligopoly would be gigantic. The mass food production paradigm is one that seems very ingrained and difficult to move away from.

14. Unsustainable production: conclusions

This has been an attempt to show that far from the mass production of cars being essentially the work of a single man or company, namely Ford (still a widespread belief), in reality it evolved out of the complex bundling of two sets of core technologies – the mass production of key mechanical components, notably the internal combustion engine, on the one hand; and the all-steel body on the other – with a third bundle of 'softer' innovations centred around how to create a mass market for the products that could now be mass produced: General Motors' contribution under Sloan. While the Ford and GM contributions have been the subject of considerable scrutiny in the past – although perhaps not along these conceptual lines – the significance of the all-steel body has been less well understood. Where the present account expands on what literature is available in this area (e.g. Nieuwenhuis and Wells, 2007; Wynn-Williams, 2009), is in further highlighting the significance of the unibody, which saw the centre of gravity in mass-produced body technology shift from North America to Europe.

In addition, the present analysis attempts to show the impact of these three bundles of innovations on the world's oldest car industry, that of France, where we see a combination of, on the one hand, firms that are among the first to embrace the new technologies – Citroën, and also Renault – and on the other, those who resist for various reasons, notably the manufacturers of traditional 'grandes routières'. The failure of the latter appears to be primarily due to their adherence to handmade engine technology, as we can also point to the survival of small firms that have not adopted all-steel, but opted for using mass-produced engines (e.g. Morgan in the UK), and – as in the case of Facel – those who managed to introduce Budd-style body construction for low-volume applications, but who used outsourced mass-produced engines to ensure a viable business model.

In all this, the managerial expertise of the key players is a given. This innovation, highlighted by Chandler (1977) is significant and all the major drivers of the bundled innovations that underpin the mass car production paradigm, Henry Ford, Edward Budd, Alfred Sloan and André Citroën, were able to build on previous managerial experience in large companies. Taylorism similarly can be assumed, as it was being established in most larger firms by the beginning of the period under discussion (1910–1940), while alternative practices with similar effectiveness also co-existed with Taylorism, notably in France (Cohen, 2001).

In summary, then, Ford turned the manufacture of Edwardian vehicles into a mass production process, enabling the mass production of key components and subassemblies such as – most importantly – engines. Budd enabled the mass production of car bodies and subsequently the introduction of unibody construction. The US, and then Europe, adopted Budd all-steel technology, taking the further step of moving to unitary construction. This then became the new model for mass producing cars, largely emulated elsewhere, including Japan, South Korea and, more recently, China. Unitary construction is still spreading. with SUVs gradually moving from body-on-frame to chassis-less monocoque construction.

Although what has been termed 'Buddism', as part of the bundle that also included Fordism and Sloanism, served the industry well while it was trying to put the world on wheels, in the more-developed countries market forces now undermine this mass production paradigm. Markets now expect much shorter product cycles, as well as more visible differentiation, leading to more diverse product ranges (Lamoreaux et al., 2002; Nieuwenhuis and Wells, 2009; Wells and Morreau, 2009). These pressures mean lower volumes per model and thus loss of economies of scale. Attempts to recapture the economies of scale needed for profitable Fordist and Buddist-style car-making are behind the industry's more recent efforts to globalise and consolidate, as well as its 'platform' strategies. These more recent developments in mass production are explored below.

Our discussion of mass food production has attempted to shed light on its roots and its implications from a technological and socio-economic perspective. The ecological and social costs of globalised food systems are huge and the consumer disconnect with food provenance in much of the Western world contributes to rendering them invisible. Can we move away from the mass-produced food paradigm and its accompanying system? This seems quite difficult and uncertain, and it would require radical systemic transformations, in particular in the form of challenging the power of large food corporations. Nonetheless we have already started to see 'rebellious' movements emerge over the last decades around slow food, the promotion of gardening, the renewed interest in local food markets and co-operatives, vegetable box schemes and short food supply chains/alternative food networks. All of these imply a renewed connection with agriculture and rural landscapes, and between consumers and the provenance of their food (Wilk, 2006; Sonnino and Marsden, 2006). The current pandemic has served to highlight the cracks in existing food systems, particularly around ecological impact, equitable access and the disparities between urban and rural populations. We have seen in part a move towards more local food consumption, hence supporting local food production. Many have posed the question of what constitutes a resilient food system? We discuss some of this in more detail elsewhere in the book. Overall, food has been a huge topic during the pandemic and we are yet to see whether it will serve to support radical long-lasting change.

PART III

Supply webs: linking production and consumption

15. Toyotism: mass production adopts supply-chain thinking

Toyotism is the term often used for the widespread adoption of the Toyota Production System, also known as 'lean production'. Key features include a re-evaluation of processes throughout the value chain, combined with the changes in labour practices that it introduced (Aoki, 2015). As mentioned previously, Budd-style mass production of bodies proved very amenable to automation. Thus we see, over time, a gradual but steady replacing of labour with capital. The car industry today produces more cars per person per year as a result of this. It also means that in most developed car-making countries fewer people are employed in car production than a few decades ago, despite higher production levels – productivity has thus improved as a result of capital investments (Andera, 2007); a trend replicated in other industries.

The equipment needed to make engines, transmissions and, especially, bodies is very expensive. This proved a large hurdle and greatly increased entry costs to car manufacturing. After World War II, Japan was occupied by the US, and Japanese car-makers had an opportunity to visit US car plants. While they were impressed with what they saw, they also realised the cost of these systems was very high and thought about ways in which the equipment could be used more intensively, thus making it more cost-effective. This move, led by Toyota, looked at the Ford–Budd system and the local manufacturers then thought of ways of taking out what they perceived as waste, or *muda*, thereby reducing cost. Toyota's novel approach became known as the Toyota Production System (TPS), was popularised as 'lean production' (Womack et al., 1990) and broadened to be relevant to other sectors of the economy, including the service sector, as 'lean thinking' (Womack and Jones, 1996).

Although initially kept within Toyota, the secrets of the TPS gradually spread as Toyota was forced to take over other manufacturers, such as Hino and Daihatsu, while it also – of necessity – had to disseminate the system throughout its supply chain. Principles such as just-in-time (JIT) and total quality management (TQM) require the co-operation of the entire value chain. This did mean that the TPS became more widely known and spread throughout the car industry, starting with Toyota's Japanese competitors, then followed by the Americans, led by Ford, and from there to European car-makers. Thus, gradually the whole car industry adopted lean production, or at least as many elements of it as they could manage. In the process Toyota lost some of its competitive advantage.

It is important to understand automobility as a system, for changing some key aspects of the system can radically alter the system as a whole. This is the case, for example, if we change the core technologies outlined above – the all-steel body and the internal combustion engine – as with the current shift to electric powertrain. For much of the twentieth century, the world car industry was dominated by US manufacturers and their global networks, notably Ford and GM, and to a lesser extent, Chrysler. There was no doubt that the American model in the automotive industry was dominant on the global stage. Recent crises at the once 'Big 3' (GM, Ford, Chrysler) combined with the collapse or near-collapse of many of their major suppliers, particularly around the financial crisis of 2008, have undermined this dominance and have led to a questioning of the business model that underpins it (Nieuwenhuis and Wells, 2009; Wells, 2010, 2013; Nieuwenhuis and Wells, 2015). The small number of players and large home market ensured that North America became one of the few locations where genuine economies of scale in car-making could be achieved using the Ford–Budd system; it became the true home of mass production; however, as the market shares of the Detroit 3 were eroded by imports and foreign transplant operations in the US, it became increasingly difficult to achieve these economies of scale.

15.1   BUDDISM IN CRISIS?

Despite the success of the Budd system throughout most of the twentieth century, in the established car markets, Buddist mass car-making can now be said to be in crisis. Profitability has been declining for decades. The performance of General Motors illustrates this decline in profitability. In the late 1920s GM's net profit margin approached 20 per cent, yet by 2000 this had fallen to only 2.7 per cent (Haglund, 2001). General Motors posted record losses and may have been technically bankrupt even before the recession of 2008–2009, but was, as the phrase goes, simply 'too big to fail'. This marginal profitability is not atypical for the volume end of car-making, although specialist producers such as BMW are still able to maximise their return through 'cost recovery', leveraging the value of their brands (Williams et al., 1994). BMW is even able to practise this approach on relatively high volumes, making it one of the most profitable firms in the industry with a return on sales typically in the 8–10 per cent range or even higher.

It is clear that the present structure of the industry and its dominant business model are so closely linked with the adoption of Budd all-steel technology that any significant change will be possible only with the adoption of a different set of core technologies and an alternative business model by the automotive industry. Through adopting mass production, car manufacturing has gradually become more efficient. This is seen as a good thing. However, there is an increasing realisation that this drive for efficiency may not make the system more resilient (Walker and Salt, 2006). Walker and Salt (2006) explain that, on the whole, humans favour efficiency, which seems preferable from various perspectives, such as simplicity, perceived more efficient use of resources, hence lower cost, etc. However, this same efficiency does make any system more vulnerable to change and external impact. They explain that although optimisation is about efficiency, it tends to be 'applied to a narrow range of values and a particular set of interests, the result is major inefficiencies in the way we generate value for societies' (ibid.: 7). Being efficient in this sense leads to the elimination of redundancies. We tend to keep only that which we perceive to be directly and immediately useful. Yet when the operating environment changes, other things may be more useful; and these may be the very things we have discarded in our quest for efficiency. It is for this reason that it leads to a steady loss of resilience (Nieuwenhuis and Lämmgård, 2013; Nieuwenhuis, 2014). In the shift to alternative powertrain, automated vehicles and shared mobility, this lack of resilience may prove problematic for the mass production car industry, ill-prepared for such a transformation.

At a basic level this can be seen in the way in which the mass production system interfaces with the market. Here is an area of tension whereby the mass production system favours efficiency through a lack of diversity, while consumers, i.e. markets, favour diversity. The attraction of moving into new markets is that newly motorising countries tend to demand automobility – virtually at any cost, but particularly they are willing to forgo diversity in favour of standardised basic automobility, at least temporarily. As markets mature, they demand and expect greater diversity – this tendency towards diversity being entirely natural in the broadest sense (Nieuwenhuis, 2014) – and as a result profits decline, because efficiency declines and costs rise. However, resilience may well increase as a result. During the 1990s, the academic proponents of 'lean' also became aware of this at some level and many of them started to promote the concept of 'agility'. It came to be recognised that while some activities along a value chain were best done 'lean', in other areas, particularly those close to the market, agility was required, which led to the coining of the term 'leagile'.

15.2   LEAN VERSUS AGILE

Essentially, while lean was regarded as the answer for all supply chains at one stage (Womack et al., 1990), it was found that tensions could rise where some supply chains interface with markets. An overview of these developments was provided by Moyano-Fuentes and Sacristán-Díaz (2011). In view of some of the limitations of lean discovered in the literature by these authors, it was concluded that for certain supply chains and certain markets, a more agile approach was required, which at times could undermine the 'leanness' of that supply chain. The questions then became:

(1)   How could lean and agile elements be combined within a single supply chain?
(2)   At what point in that supply chain should the change from lean to agile be made?

The latter became known as the 'decoupling point'. The 'decoupling point' concept was first mooted by Hoekstra and Romme (1992), and defined as 'The point in the product axis to which the customer's order penetrates. It is where order driven and forecast driven activities meet.'

Later, Mason-Jones and Towill (1999) argued that there are at least two pipelines within the supply chain – material flow and information flow – and both flows have their own separate decoupling points. Therefore, they introduced the concept of 'material decoupling point' and 'information decoupling point'. This 'material decoupling point' resonates with the 'decoupling point' proposed by Hoekstra and Romme (1992). Mason-Jones and Towill (1999) defined the 'information decoupling point' as 'the point in the information pipeline to which the marketplace order data penetrates without modification. It is where market driven and forecast driven information flows meet.' Thus, over time, two types of decoupling point came to be identified: the material decoupling point and the information decoupling point.

The understanding is then that upstream from the decoupling point, processes are operated on lean principles – inventory is held in generic form and the final configuration is only performed when the customer order is received – while downstream from the decoupling point, the agile principle is applied. Christopher and Towill (2001) stated that this approach can be applied when there is a possibility of modular design in product architecture. This resonates with aspects of the automotive value chain whereby generic subassemblies such as powertrain can be made by large facilities in order to achieve the desired economies of scale via lean processes. These are then supplied to assembly plants, which combine them in a variety of more flexible processes.

Several factors impact on the position of the material decoupling point. On the one hand, it depends on the longest lead time the end customer is prepared to tolerate (Naylor et al., 1999; Mason-Jones and Towill, 1999; Childerhouse and Towill, 2000; Mason-Jones et al., 2000). On the other hand, its position depends on the product variety and variability in demand. An increase in product variety and fluctuating volume of demand would force the material decoupling point to move upstream, which makes the supply chain more 'agile'. In contrast, a more stable business environment with lower product variety and stable demand would move the material decoupling point downstream, making the supply chain 'leaner' (Krishnamurthy and Yauch, 2007).

Naylor et al. (1999) argued that a 'postponement' strategy contributes to moving the material decoupling point closer to the end customer, thereby increasing both the efficiency and responsiveness of the supply chain. Postponement here refers to delayed configuration of the product or product/service offering; the final assembly does not take place until customer orders are received (Christopher and Towill, 2000). Similarly, Childerhouse and Towill (2000) define postponement as the application of the material decoupling point before the point of product differentiation. A core element behind the postponement strategy is modular design. Feitzinger and Lee (1997) proposed two concepts: 'modular product design' and 'modular process design'. Modular product design refers to dividing the entire product into several sub-modules, and redesigning modules with standardised interfaces so that sub-modules can be easily assembled together, which enables components to be manufactured separately and even in parallel and one component can be shared by different products. Similarly, modular process design refers to breaking down the complete production process into several simple independent sub-processes that can function together as a whole, thus, the production sub-processes can be performed separately or can be resequenced. On the same basis, some processes can be performed in-house, while others can be outsourced, with this mix changing over time. Modularity enables a company to assemble standard components in the earlier stages of production and delay assembling the components that differentiate the products.

Postponement strategies contribute to leanness as well as agility. On the one hand, by delaying product differentiation, the supply chain produces standard semi-finished products as long as possible. Product differentiation then occurs at the material decoupling point; the generic inventory is regarded as strategic stock. In this way, only differentiated processes cause delay, which greatly reduces the lead time from the order placement by customers to product delivery. It increases the responsiveness of the supply chain. This has been behind the drive towards modular supply in the automotive industry, whereby so-called 'module suppliers', who sit conceptually even above 'tier one' suppliers (or have become the new tier one suppliers) no longer supply components, but comprehensive modules that are designed to interface with each other in the assembly process. Smart's facility in Hambach, France, is probably one of the best examples of this approach, resulting in a final assembly process that only takes around five hours, compared with 15–40 hours for a typical car final assembly process, depending on product complexity and production efficiency. Thus, over time, the areas that mass car producers have considered part of their activities have shifted, as illustrated in Figure 15.1.

Figure 15.1 shows how Ford initially captured much of the upstream value chain, even owning and operating forests and timber processing plants for pre-Budd body structures, iron ore mines, rubber plantations in Brazil, etc. However, Ford stopped short of engaging in the retail end. Initially, no suppliers existed who could supply in the volumes Ford needed for its mass production. By the 1920s this had changed, allowing GM and Chrysler in particular to move away from bringing primary sourcing in-house, but GM also moved more into activities beyond the factory gate, such as vehicle finance, of which Ford disapproved. Moving on a century, then, we find that more upstream activities are subcontracted to these module suppliers, while original equipment manufacturers (OEMs – which in the automotive industry somewhat confusingly indicates the ultimate car manufacturer, such as Ford or Fiat) have moved further into the market by being more involved in retail, distribution and

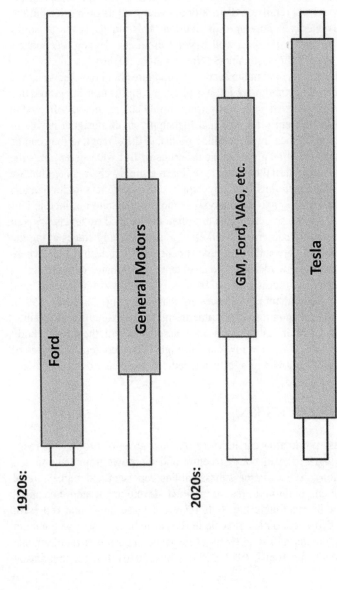

Figure 15.1   Part of the value chain captured by mass production firms

finance. An even more extreme case is Tesla, which has almost moved back to where Ford was, with the exception of mining for primary materials. However, Tesla's novel business and manufacturing model involves battery production, virtually all assembly supplies, such as seats (Ford also makes these, but most manufacturers subcontract seats), but Tesla also covers retail and distribution, owning all its own sales outlets, as well as energy supply and distribution. This makes Tesla unusually vertically integrated, going well beyond the areas 'legacy' car-makers consider as part of their business (Nieuwenhuis, 2018b).

Little is actually said in the academic literature about the precise nature of the material decoupling point; it is often, by implication, suggested that greater freedom exists in reconfiguring supply chains than is reflected in reality. It is frequently implied that the supply chain designer has complete freedom in locating decoupling points, to the extent that they can be manipulated for strategic or tactical purposes. But what determines the location of the material decoupling point in a supply chain, and what are therefore the constraints faced by supply chain designers and managers in managing this point? The analysis of the Budd system outlined in Part II suggests that these constraints are often determined by levels of fixed investment in the equipment used at various processing stages along the supply chain. Where such fixed investments are high, lean is best, where they are low, agile works well. To an extent this resonates with the notion of modularity in processes, whereby some processes are more amenable to agility, while others are of necessity lean (Feitzinger and Lee, 1997). Thus in modern automotive manufacturing, to the extent this is feasible, those high-capital investment processes associated with the all-steel body tend to be lean, while the low-capital, high-labour content processes of final assembly allow the agility needed to interface flexibly with the market.

15.3 CONCLUSIONS

In the mass production car industry, the key areas of production focus are the integrated steel body structure and the powertrain (engine and transmission). These major subassemblies represent the highest level of investment both in terms of product development and in capital investment in manufacturing. It is therefore these areas that represent both the key to economies of scale in the car industry, but also the main barriers to greater agility in terms of response to customer requirements (Nieuwenhuis and Wells, 1997, 2003; Wells, 2010). It is for this reason that while customers often have access to a broad range of colour and trim variations, for example, their choice in terms of powertrain and body style is restricted, despite the now widespread adoption of platform strategies, modular supply and concerted attempts at 'mass customisation' (Alford et al., 2000; Doran et al., 2007; Brabazon et al., 2010). It is also typically the case in mass car production that both the body and powertrain areas remain within the realm of the final assembler, the OEM. For these reasons, much of Toyota's innovative work was focused on the area of body production – press shop, body-in-white, and paint, as these are the least amenable to flexibility (Womack et al., 1990).

This also means that the car mass production system – and by extension that in many other industries – is still essentially supply driven; emphasising once again that with a supply-driven system, demand is to a large extent driven by supply in order to satisfy the manufacturing systems that need a return on the very high investments required in order to supply in the volumes that were once essential to meet demand and which therefore demand that level of supply to break even. In this context, reducing demand in a move towards more sustainable consumption and production is to all intents and purposes a non-starter, as the implications for some of the largest players in the economy are too awful to contemplate; these firms have become 'too big to fail'. However, one way of breaking through this barrier to greater agility may be by moving to a more modular design approach, as suggested in some of the decoupling point literature (Feitzinger and Lee, 1997), and then moving the decoupling point for these key assemblies further up the supply chain, for example by outsourcing engines, and/or outsourcing body/chassis. Another method may be to move to a different type of technology that allows break-even at much lower economies of scale, such as by abandoning 'Budd-style' all-steel body construction for a different solution (Nieuwenhuis and Wells, 2003, 2007; Nieuwenhuis, 2014; Nieuwenhuis, 2018a). Some of these notions will be explored later.

16. Building sustainable supply chains

16.1 SUSTAINABLE SUPPLY CHAIN MANAGEMENT: ITS CENTRALITY AND SHORTCOMINGS

Economists are increasingly forced to accept that economics has to work within environmental constraints. Other established business disciplines find themselves equally challenged. With the ongoing advances of environmental approaches, some form of ecological approach to business analysis has the potential to put increasing pressure on many of these older disciplines. It is a first step towards this newer thinking that is proposed in this chapter. Recent work by Gruner and Power (2017) extended industrial ecology (IE) specifically to supply chain management (SCM), while Winn and Pogutz (2013) working from a combined organisation and ecology perspective also specifically identify SCM as playing a key role here. The reason for relating these concepts to SCM is that SCM, by its very nature, permeates economic activity at many levels and can thus be considered the very 'lifeblood' of economic activity, while at the same time impacting on many different ecosystems, yet very few serious attempts have been made – as far as we are aware – to cast SCM into any type of ecological model. In addition, as outlined in the previous chapter, the moves towards 'lean' and subsequently 'agile' and 'leagile' have put supply chains at the heart of the SCP equation and its 'problematic'.

SCM has started to recognise this key role and has developed the subdiscipline of Sustainable SCM, or SSCM in response. Yet, it could be argued that for many years SSCM itself has been working in splendid isolation; making reference more to the SCM literature than to the steadily advancing literature in sustainable business or sustainability in general – true also for the wider academic literature on corporate sustainability. However, recently there have been signs of greater synergies between these two fields and some publications now suggest that both the wider sustainable business literature (Winn and Pogutz, 2013; Hahn et al., 2017; Tregidga et al., 2018) and the SSCM literature are beginning to link with current thinking in sustainability and business (Montabon et al., 2016; Matthews et al., 2016). The present contribution attempts to build on this by linking SSCM thinking with the newly emerging literature of business resilience based on ecological principles, putting a stake in the ground for a possible new sub-field of 'ecological' supply chain management (ESCM) which could be used to leverage true sustainability thinking into other business disciplines.

Sustainable development is a complex phenomenon that represents unparalleled challenges for business and business researchers alike. It is a highly cosmopolitan problem requiring the forging of connections across national borders, between sectors, e.g. business and the third sector (i.e. voluntary sector), and across academic disciplines (Beck, 2010; Hajer, 1997; Urry, 2011). Hence, sustainability requires thinking beyond the boundaries of a single entity or organisation to consider entire value chains and production and consumption systems (Lebel and Lorek, 2008). This puts supply chains (SCs) and supply chain management (SCM) at the heart of the policy and practice agenda for sustainability, especially in the context of SCP. Over the last five years, many literature reviews of SSCM have been conducted (Abbasi and Nilsson, 2012; Carter and Easton, 2011; Ashby et al., 2012; Carter and Rogers, 2008; Miemczyk et al., 2012; Touboulic and Walker, 2015), taking stock of research in the field and showing the growing interest for and criticality of this area to both academics and practitioners alike. It has been shown that the predominant focus has been on empirical research employing primarily surveys or positivistic case studies. As a result, a great deal of knowledge has been accumulated on what practices companies are actually implementing as well as enablers and inhibitors. Both internal (e.g. capabilities) and external factors (e.g. collaboration with suppliers) have been identified. Not surprisingly these are factors already prominent in other areas of the SCM literature (e.g. technology adoption) making SSCM appear to be just another 'innovation' promoting and reinforcing the objective of supply chain efficiency. In addition, such studies are often limited by the understanding of sustainability of those surveyed, which rarely reflects current thinking, thereby limiting true progress. This perception is further reinforced by the attention paid to exploring the links between some aspects of a narrow sustainability framework (such as eco-efficiency and social responsibility) and firms' financial performance (Thornton et al., 2013; Wong, 2013) in pursuit of that illusive 'triple bottom line' (TBL). As pointed out by Pagell and Shevchenko (2014) not much has been done to understand 'how' SSCM happens. In addition, the vast majority of these authors point to the alarming lack of theory in the field, and the limited attempts at theory building. Given the strong focus on empirical, positivist studies in this area, this represents a significant shortcoming, which calls into question the relevance of empirical findings with such a weak theoretical basis.

We contend here that the main challenge to the development of SSCM theory – along with other business disciplines – lies in the difficulty that researchers face in dealing with the intrinsic complexity and interdisciplinarity of the notion of sustainability and its fundamental concern with accommodating human activities within broader natural systems and over longer time spans. On the one hand, there is the view that sustainability cannot be achieved at the micro-level, as sustainable development is a macro-level concept (Ehrenfeld, 2009), while it is also argued that it is not supported by current political economic structures and discourses which are generally geared towards growth despite the costs (i.e. real costs externalised to society and/or to future generations), combined with a general unwillingness to engage with the science behind issues such as climate change, planetary boundaries, etc.; a problematic that is explored in areas like sustainable consumption and production (SCP) (Jackson, 2009), or the 'de-growth' movement (Georgescu-Roegen et al., 1979; Kallis et al., 2012). These literatures challenge the dominance of the current economic growth principle as embodied in the existing economic model, which, it is argued, promotes increasing levels of inequality (Piketty, 2013) and the uneconomic liquidation of natural capital (Czech, 2013; Daly, 1996; Dietz and O'Neill, 2013). On this basis the only sustainable supply chain is the one that does not exist. On the other hand, there is a school of thought that sustainability must be built simultaneously from the bottom up and the top down (Meadows et al., 2005).

From the paradigmatic literature of the 1990s, the SSCM field took the theories that most closely resembled its own concerns with competitive advantage, namely NRBV (Natural Resource Based View) (Hart, 1995) and the triple bottom line (TBL), rather than the more challenging theoretical lenses offered by ecocentrism (Shrivastava, 1995; Starik, 1995), sustainocentrism (Gladwin et al., 1995) and the theory of the ecologically sustainable organisation (Starik and Rands, 1995). It has been recognised that the goal of harm reduction places an artificial upper limit on environmental performance (Pagell and Shevchenko, 2014) and thereby limits the extent to which the environment can be said to win from what are merely reductions in unsustainability. In contrast, sustainable development would require firms and their supply chains to have a net positive effect on the natural environment (Pagell and Shevchenko, 2014). Unfortunately, the field's lack of engagement with ecology and ecology-influenced sustainability research means that we have little notion of what a more positive contribution might look like, e.g. the restoration of natural capital (Hawken et al., 1999). Secondly, there is increased recognition that social and environmental improvements simply will not always pay back in economic terms (Orsato, 2009; Awaysheh and Klassen, 2010; Wang and Sarkis, 2013). Still, often due to external pressures (Wang and Sarkis, 2013) firms will have no choice but to make such investments regardless of whether they pay or not (Pagell and Shevchenko, 2014).

Ecocentrism questions the very notion that the environment is little more than an object that needs to be managed (Gladwin et al., 1995). Natural capital has an intrinsic value as well as the instrumental value of providing the foundations of our economic and social subsystems: 'ecosystem services'. Shrivastava (1995) argues that the management researcher should try to represent the natural environment as a stakeholder in its own right. In a major departure from the discourse of eco-efficiency, sustainability is thus constructed as a moral question for practitioners and researchers alike. The ecocentric paradigm also forces us to question one of the most taken-for-granted assumptions that underpin eco-efficiency: how firms make their profits in the first place. Firms are able to make profits because they, and their suppliers, do not pay anything like a fair price for the environmental destruction that their economic activity is responsible for – these costs are 'externalised' to society and/or future generations. The 'economic world view' (Krebs, 2008), with its competitive and economic growth paradigm, thus dominates the SSCM landscape and it is difficult for theoreticians in this field to go beyond such traditional perspectives, which have been strongly influenced by neoclassical economics and the concept of 'the business of business is business' (Friedman, 1970), even though sustainability issues may require a more radical shift in mindsets and business models. This could allow transitioning to new conceptions of consumption and the purpose of the firm, as well as developing alternatives to the dominant discourse of growth. In reality, SSCM research to date has been primarily focused on economic and environmental aspects and has not addressed the full complexity of systemic sustainability research and yet it would have a key role to play in any system transition.

Most SSCM research has focused on what practices would be most effective in achieving environmental and social performance with suppliers, without compromising on profitability (Pagell and Shevchenko, 2014) and without questioning the very nature of particular supply chains and the extent to which what they supply and how they supply it are themselves 'sustainable' (Van Bommel, 2011). In particular, the literature has emphasised the issue of how companies should screen and select their suppliers against their social and environmental requirements. And yet, the implementation of social and environmental practices cannot be reduced to problems of screening and selection and there is a need to investigate how buyers are dealing with long-term legacy suppliers (Hoejmose and Adrien-Kirby, 2012). Furthermore, Pagell and Shevchenko (2014) point out that current research in the field has failed to fully capture all of a supply chain's impacts, i.e. economic, social and environmental, mainly because of a theoretical distortion in favour of profit maximisation and economically beneficial practices under the guise of TBL. It has been argued that organisational sustainability can only be fully achieved if sustainability issues are addressed at the SC level (Preuss, 2005; Paulraj, 2011) as they bring together a multiplicity of actors in different locations and have an impact at multiple levels (Park-Poaps and Rees, 2010). SC activities are a critical source of value and competitive advantage for businesses (Burgess et al., 2006); thus an organisation's environmental and social performance is affected by that of its suppliers (Tate et al., 2010). Simpson and Power (2005) have shown that supply relationships present the only way for business to influence the sustainability of products and services.

SCs are made up of both formal quantifiable mechanisms of production and complex social interactions. Each SC is unique, composed of an idiosyncratic collective of actors shaping their own micro-systems within the macro structure of the chain. The very nature of SSCs suggests that a comprehensive understanding of their dynamics must account for their social complexity, their historical baggage and ambiguous causalities. SSCs are highly embedded in context, and understanding of the SSC emerges in local situations and through specific interactions between buyers and suppliers as well as other actors in the network (Gold et al., 2010). While specific initiatives have been introduced, the actual transition towards a more sustainable SC is not like a traditional organisational change initiative, which is finite and introduced over a specific period of time. This transition is continuous, emergent and is embedded within a broader movement, i.e. not bounded by the organisational realm, but about reframing the relationship between society and the natural environment (Paulraj, 2011; Peattie, 2011). Carter and Rogers (2008) note that economic, social and environmental objectives are interdependent and organisations must make the link between them. Within organisations, as well as in the wider society, this therefore requires a fundamental culture change. These aspects demonstrate that SSCM should be transformational because its implementation questions the status quo (Linton et al., 2007; Seuring et al., 2008; Fabbe-Costes et al., 2011). SSCM is also relational because it takes into account not only intra- and interorganisational relationships but also relationships with society as a whole and the links between SC operations and the natural environment.

Much of the perceived complexity of the sustainability concept probably centres on the very concept of the triple bottom line. This was in reality never part of the original sustainable development definition, as framed by the Brundtland Commission (WCED, 1987), which focused instead on our responsibility to future generations and North–South equity. In fact, by presenting sustainability as constituting the economic, the social and the environmental, the focus has been more on current concerns, as these three areas in reality can be dealt with at a current operational level, while sustainability, as presented by the WCED (1987), very much emphasises responsibility to future generations, which moves it much more into the realm of the longer-term strategic. In fact, separating the economic, social and, indeed, environmental once again from the sustainability concept may therefore be much more helpful in redirecting that primary focus back onto the future generations issue. The economic, social and environmental can then be framed as more immediate concerns, thereby necessitating more immediate action, while sustainability becomes a more overarching idea informing these elements on a strategic level, rather than constituting them as suggested by the triple bottom line concept. We will start to explore how such a shift can be brought about in the next chapter.

17. Learning from natural supply systems: towards ecological supply chain management

Given the issues outlined in the previous chapter, with TBL as its primary aim, this still leaves us with the economic as the primary focus of business and of SCM, including SSCM. It is clear now that, at its best, SSCM should challenge this 'economic worldview' to which Krebs (2008) offers an alternative 'ecological worldview'. Though the detail is missing, it becomes evident from a study of the ecological literature that such a worldview is already in many respects implied by that ecological literature. As outlined in the introduction, some suggestions have been made by ecologists of how this thinking could be linked with business thinking, while attempts in the business literature to engage with the ecological literature are also on the increase (e.g. Field and Conn, 2007; Whiteman et al., 2013; Winn and Pogutz, 2013). It is clear, that if SSCM is to live up to the 'sustainable' parts of its name, it has to engage with such thinking, something also strongly suggested by Winn and Pogutz (2013).

Gruner and Power (2017) provide a recent contribution that attempts to link ecological concepts with SSCM. They take the ecological concept of intergradation to show how sustainability thinking can gradually be merged with SCM thinking. This concept describes how different species of plants gradually merge at the boundaries of their ranges, rather than presenting a sudden transition from one ecosystem to the other. Based on this concept they present a number of principles that can be used to guide any moves towards more sustainable SC, notably locality – favouring the local and decentralised; steady state – aiming for closed loop systems; gradualism – aiming for slow and steady change, rather than sudden change (see also the ideas explored from the consumption perspective in Part I); interdependence, and heterogeneity. This final principle of Gruner and Power's 'intergradation principles', that of 'heterogeneity', derives from the ecological concept of biodiversity. This is probably a much more central concept than these authors suggest and is certainly deserving of closer scrutiny in the context of SSCM; something this analysis will therefore focus on from this point. In this respect we propose taking a further step. While Winn and Pogutz (2013: 205) clearly distinguish between seeing organisations within their natural environment, as opposed to using ecological concepts as analogies for organisations, it is suggested here that the latter can be leveraged to enable organisations – in our case businesses – to better understand their embeddedness within ecosystems and thus to bring about a gradual shift in understanding and corporate behaviour more in line with that understanding. In fact, we would argue that such an approach would contribute in achieving their concept of 'organizational ecosystem embeddedness' (Winn and Pogutz, 2013: 220). In this respect, we agree with Winn and Pogutz (2013) that the concept of diversity is potentially very useful.

17.1   THE DIVERSITY CONCEPT

Industrial ecology, through its notion of industrial symbiosis and its iconic concept of eco-industrial parks featuring ecosystem-like symbiosis among different industrial processes (Frosch and Gallopoulos, 1989; Heeres et al., 2004), already promotes the concept of diversity: only if the members of a group of firms are diverse enough for the output of the processes of one to provide inputs into the processes of others can an idealised industrial symbiosis situation be brought about. This is an SCM issue and an SSCM issue, but is also central to ecology and biology (Meadows, 2009). Diversity arises naturally, in part through spontaneous mutation and also because species operate in niches; each species has a so-called 'fundamental' niche, which denotes the maximum niche that species could occupy in terms of climate, resources, etc. in the absence of competition (Krebs, 2008). With competition, that species occupies its 'realised' niche, which is a subset of its fundamental niche. It is no different in economies; without competition, a company can occupy an entire market, i.e. it holds a monopoly position. In reality, in a competitive market environment, companies operate within their realised niches, which can vary over time depending on that competitive environment.

Bejan and Zane (2012) give the example of a forest floor, which combines tree canopies of varying size such that few spaces are left empty. In an established forest, the larger trees' canopies cover most of the area, but there is room for smaller trees' canopies in between and yet smaller ones in the spaces left between their canopies and those of the bigger trees, while smaller, lower plants occupy the even smaller spaces in between, forming the 'undergrowth'. All have access to light, water and other resources according to their size, but there is room for all. In markets the same applies; in the car market, for example, mass volume producers such as GM, Toyota or VW cover the major share of the market, followed by specialist mass producers such as BMW, Mercedes or Volvo, and followed by smaller specialist producers such as Ferrari or Porsche. The even-smaller spaces in between are taken up by the likes of Morgan, Pagani and Karma. In a saturated community, all niches are filled, while in an unsaturated community not all niches are filled, so there is the potential for an invader, such as Tesla, to come in (Krebs, 2008). In certain animals the equivalent is their home range or territory (Odum, 1959).

The concept of diversity, then, is based on that of biodiversity – the notion that a healthy ecosystem relies on the interaction of a number of different species (Molles, 2005). This needs more exploration, for despite widespread concern in conservation circles about loss of biodiversity, the need for diversity has not always been accepted as fundamental. In fact, it can be said to have emerged as recently as the 1980s (Tilman, 2000; McCann, 2000; Lévêque and Mounolou, 2001). Tilman reviewed the relevant literature and concluded that, usually, greater diversity leads to greater productivity in plant communities, greater nutrient retention and greater ecosystem stability (Tilman, 2000). In fact, he quotes research which shows that each halving of the number of plant species leads to a 10–20 per cent loss of productivity within a given plot. Recent findings also suggest that diversity may increase where and when there is greater environmental variability, i.e. in a more changeable environment (Holmes, 2013). This suggests that natural systems may prepare for such environmental instability, in order to be able to respond to it relatively quickly – it adds resilience. It is now widely accepted that loss of biodiversity can be damaging and is certainly undesirable. It was also recognised at the 1992 Rio Earth Summit that little was known and understood about biodiversity (Quarrie, 1992).

The resulting drive to research the concept has had the effect that diversity is beginning to be regarded as desirable in a wider context and in recent years an increasing number of observers has attempted to apply the principle to social, economic and industrial structures. Diversity in ecosystems comes into its own at times of change (Geng and Côté, 2007). Diversity implies that for any given stable ecosystem there is a certain degree of apparent redundancy – the presence of species with no obviously relevant role in the system (Peterson et al., 1998). It is precisely in this respect that the concept may embody lessons for business, particularly in the context of SCM, where traditionally 'efficiency' has been pursued as a primary objective. Is it possible that this pursuit of efficiency – while laudable in many respects – has in fact made supply chains – and economies – less resilient? This point is made by Walker and Salt (2006) who challenge directly the notion of 'efficiency' and instead highlight the important role of redundancy in order to achieve resilient systems. Industrial evolution has gradually led to greater efficiency in our systems; however, as Walker and Salt have argued, this efficiency has also in many cases led to a reduction in system resilience. Walker and Salt (2006) further point out that the response to external threats – the 2008 recession for example – from many decision makers has been to advocate greater efficiency, although in fact, greater resilience may be required, especially if a move towards more sustainable production – and hence consumption – is seriously on the agenda. This may be even more relevant now, in the wake of the Covid-19 crisis. Peterson et al. (1998) explain that any change may push an ecosystem to reorganise suddenly around a set of alternative 'mutually reinforcing processes'; a 'tipping point' is reached that leads to a different set of operating conditions and, they argue, that only a resilient system can deal with such – often dramatic – change. These authors place great emphasis on the importance of scale, whereby in a given ecosystem, a mouse operates at a different scale from a moose. Each experiences the same environment in a different way, although they may share some resources. This is the concept of hierarchies of linked adaptive systems operating at different scales; it is no different in supply chains where the role of the smaller players cannot be separated from that of the larger ones.

17.2   RESILIENCE THROUGH DIVERSITY

Each system is driven by key processes at each scale and these link up to determine the behaviour of the system as a whole. In the context of industrial symbiosis, for example, we could compare small firms that benefit from the by-products of larger players with mice and those larger producers with moose (Walker and Salt, 2006). This scale effect allows a measure of mutual reinforcement while minimising potentially harmful competition (Peterson et al., 1998). Again, in supply chains, webs or networks we can see how small specialists can share resources with larger firms whose outputs it uses without competing with them. Industrial symbiosis systems in IE are an example of this. However, despite their size, these small players help make the industrial symbiotic ecosystem more resilient, i.e. more capable of withstanding change.

In fact, this phenomenon also has advantages from a more conventional economic perspective, as companies of different size can engage in different business strategies, because their interests do not overlap (Garmestani et al., 2006). By taking this scale effect into account, what appears to be redundancy is often not (Peterson et al., 1998). In fact, as disturbances are often limited to specific scales, functions and firms operating at different scales are able to survive (Peterson et al., 1998). It is possible, for example, that a supplier hit by a disaster at a key facility may only be able to supply 20 per cent of its pre-disaster output; this may be enough to supply smaller customers, while larger customers have to idle their plants until full capacity is restored. In this way, there is no collapse of the entire supply chain, but merely a temporary reduction in supply to the market, met by some of the smaller players in an industry. This may actually be sufficient to meet demand in an immediate post-disaster phase when demand may be much reduced (Fujimoto and Park, 2014).

Others warn, however, that the loss of species – e.g. several large suppliers in an SC in this context – would reduce resilience; the system as a whole becomes more vulnerable (Peterson et al., 1998). This is true of many supply chains due to what they term 'cross-scale functional reinforcement'. Supplies by larger players to smaller firms could be such a process, the loss of which would affect several smaller firms, although if some equivalent large firms survive, the small firms may be able to re-source. The more limited the number of possible suppliers, the more vulnerable their customers. This point can be illustrated by the 'bailout' of General Motors and Chrysler by the Bush and Obama administrations in the post-2008 financial crisis. Although still resented by many in the US, it is quite clear that any collapse, of GM in particular, would have led to a collapse of much of the US automotive supply base, which in turn would have undermined the viability of surviving manufacturers, most notably Ford, while also making it near impossible for new players to emerge post-crisis. At such times, therefore, governments have a key role to play in retaining system resilience in the economy.

An important step in broadening the SSCM model is a change to thinking of industries as ecosystems and supply chains in terms of food webs. This also moves beyond the current concern of making supply chains more efficient, i.e. focusing considerable effort on doing more with less. It is easy to understand this way of thinking – on the face of it by being efficient in our use of resources we appear to be more in tune with our environment and hence more 'sustainable'. It is important to realise that this type of efficiency only applies in certain narrow circumstances and is not universally applicable. In fact, some natural processes – such as seed production in many species – appear to us very wasteful. Similarly, many human systems, like most natural systems, need a degree of redundancy ('heterogeneity' in Gruner and Power's terms (2017)) and apparent inefficiency to render them resilient and resilience is about ensuring longer-term survival, i.e. the future, future generations, or sustainability in the true sense.

17.3   SUPPLY WEBS

The term supply 'chain' is itself problematic as it forces people concep-tually into linear thinking where linear thinking is inappropriate. Whilst this approach can be defended on some levels, by instead thinking of supply systems as 'webs', analogous with food webs in ecology, we can begin to understand how they can be made more resilient. Ecology also initially thought in term of food 'chains', but observation of actual natural systems prompted the change to conceiving of most of them as 'webs' (Krebs, 2008; Nieuwenhuis, 2014: 79–80). Chains are, after all, only as strong as their weakest link, while webs are resilient; they can sustain some damage before they are rendered inoperable. So, we think in terms of supply 'chains' – where linearity is implied, and 'tiers' of suppliers, whereby one tier feeds neatly into the next one up and up until the final assembler is reached. This tiering approach is a caricature of reality even today. This thinking came from the Japanese *keiretsu* system, particularly at Toyota, which probably came closer than most supply systems to such a structure, but even there, a true pyramidal tiering structure never fully existed. Take materials suppliers, for example: providers of steel, glass, plastics or aluminium. These are likely to supply into many of these tiers, such that they operate essentially parallel to the pyramid and throughout its entire elevation; energy suppliers operate similarly. Other suppliers supply electronic sensors that find their way into an ABS system, an airbag system or an engine management system. The former applications would see the supplier of such sensors supplying into so-called tier 1 or 2 suppliers; in the last application they would deal direct with the vehicle assembler, the OEM, while they might also supply the aftermarket. So, where do they fit in a tiered structure?

In reality, supply systems are already more akin to ecological food webs than to tiered pyramids; industries consist of series of interlocking webs of relationships between firms. As part of the network there are suppliers of various kinds, relationships with other manufacturers such as memberships of trade bodies, but also more concrete arrangements such as joint development, exchange of components, or even of products. In addition, there are relationships with logistics providers, distributors, dealers, customers. In fact, network theories are also supportive of this notion (Provan and Fish, 2007). So how would diversity add resilience to a supply web? We have made an initial attempt to illustrate this in figure 17.1. Figure 17.1 shows a supply web with a range of resilience measures built in. It is illustrative of many manufacturing processes, such as car manufacturing, whereby the vehicle assembly is focused on P1 and P2 facilities, such that one can still supply vehicles even when the other one is down for some reason. In practice, each would make a mixture of vehicles with the most popular models being duplicated, while other, lower-volume models could be built in one of these facil-ities only. Similarly, each plant has a range of T1 or systems suppliers, with some duplicated, some supplying one plant (e.g. for the dedicated model built there) and others supplying both plants. For one T1 supplier the figure shows a double line to P2, indicating the use, or option to use multiple logistics routes, providers and/or modes in order to add resilience to the logistics that binds the web together. Suppliers and assembly plants would preferably be in geographically separate locations in case of unforeseen events preventing production. However, the whole supply web would be – as much as realistically possible – located within a compact regional setting, as resilience can decrease with increasing distance; the longer the distance over which supplies travel, the more can go wrong. At the same time, as was seen in the Tohoku earthquake and tsunami in Japan, too much co-location of key suppliers can also wipe out key parts of a supply chain, so again a balance needs to be struck (see below). This connects with Gruner and Power's (2017) principles of 'locality' and 'interdependence'. However, inevitably some suppliers will be located outside this regional setting and special measures would have to be added to boost the resilience of those parts of the web.

Figure 17.1 also includes those suppliers (e/m = energy/materials) who potentially supply the entire value chain, such as materials suppliers (e.g. steel, aluminium) and energy suppliers. These are also the most likely to link beyond the confines of Figure 17.1 into the natural environment and the supply of ecosystem services in terms of raw materials and energy. Similarly, at the downstream end, multiple routes to market are desirable, in case of problems with internal distribution or with external distributors

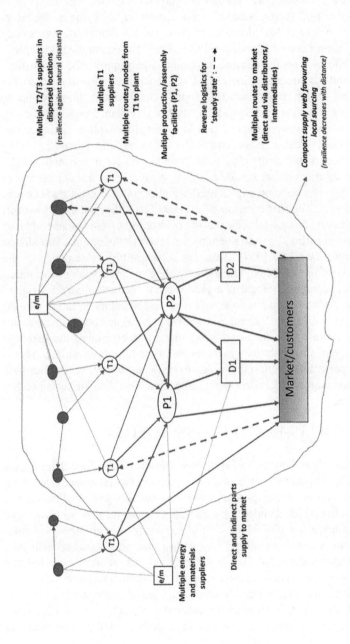

Multiple T2/T3 suppliers in dispersed locations
(resilience against natural disasters)

Multiple T1 suppliers

Multiple routes/modes from T1 to plant

Multiple production/assembly facilities (P1, P2)

Reverse logistics for 'steady state' : – – ➤

Multiple routes to market (direct and via distributors/intermediaries)

Compact supply web favouring local sourcing
(resilience decreases with distance)

Multiple energy and materials suppliers

Direct and indirect parts supply to market

Market/customers

Figure 17.1   A typical supply web in manufacturing

or dealers. Furthermore, aftermarket parts are supplied both direct from the T1 or T2/3 suppliers and via the assembler. Finally, the model incorporates a reverse logistics flow to close the loop, or create the 'steady state' mentioned by Gruner and Power (2017) as one of their principles.

While these resilience measures would largely apply to both unsustainable and sustainable supply chains, resilience itself also forms a crucial element within any sustainable supply chain model, thus 'resilience thinking' (Walker and Salt, 2006) itself will enhance understanding of how natural systems operate and how they link with human systems, prompting, ideally, more sustainable thinking and practices among practitioners and academics, with the potential for a new approach to SC to emerge that we could term *ecological supply chain management* (ESCM). The basic principles for this and the other criteria are set out in Table 17.1. The first criterion is resilience, as outlined above. However, importantly, this model separates the environment from sustainability, as explained earlier. For sustainability we revert to the original Brundtland definition (WCED, 1987). This was subsequently reinterpreted in the context of the so-called 'triple bottom line' of the social, environmental and economic. Here it is argued that this detracts from the original concept which highlights our collective responsibility to future generations and also to the 'Global South', while the triple bottom line concept refers more to the here and now, thereby undermining the essential message of sustainability, i.e. responsibility to future generations. This is an important distinction that needs to be made for SSCM, and business academia more widely, to enable full engagement with the sustainability concept.

17.4   ILLUSTRATIVE CASE: TOYOTA

An example of how lack of resilience impacts on a supply chain is provided by Toyota Motor Co. and its response to natural disasters in Japan. Toyota was heavily impacted by the Tohoku earthquake and tsunami of 2011, after which it undertook a number of measures in order to improve its resilience, some of which involved a reduction in efficiency, in order to create a degree of redundancy with a view to enhancing resilience. A detailed mapping of Toyota's supply network in Japan revealed that there were just over 500 direct suppliers in Japan, located on 1,500 sites (Matsuo, 2015). Of these, 300 were identified as single sources for some 1,000 parts based in locations considered vulnerable to natural disasters. Although the average car contains some 20,000–30,000 parts, even one

Table 17.1 ESCM criteria

Criterion	Natural or social model	Supply chain	Limitations
Resilience	One of the key elements of resilience is diversity/heterogeneity. Ecological diversity at species and system level.	• Multiple sourcing • Location of facilities • Regional supply webs favoured • Multiple routes and modes for supply • Multiple routes to market	Always a trade-off between resilience and efficiency.
Environment	This refers here to immediate environmental impacts such as noise, air and water pollution, waste, etc., recognising that some of these may be persistent in the environment, such as nuclear waste.	• Use of modes in logistics • Distances over which goods are shipped • Energy use in production and logistics • Product impacts • Production impacts • Footprint of firm, sector and web	While environmental measures are often seen as adding costs, they are increasingly used for competitive advantage. Also, crucially, they are part of the firm's 'social licence to operate'.
Society	Acknowledging the interaction between the societal and environmental levels. A systemic perspective on all stakeholders involved or affected.	• Does the SC enhance the life of all stakeholders? • Do all members of the supply web have a social licence to operate?	Responsibility for CSR extends both up and down the supply chain.

Criterion	Natural or social model	Supply chain	Limitations
Economy	The central aspect considered here is survivability for organisations to fulfil their social role.	• Can all members of the value chain cover their costs?	In a sustainability based model, there may be no need for firms to be consistently profitable; break-even is sufficient, as firms fulfil primarily a social role.
Sustainability	Responsibility to future generations.	• Does the SC benefit both present and future generations? • Does the product or service fulfil a need or a want?	Idealistic criteria not always realistic; often a laudable aim, rather than realistic business model. However, longer term thinking needs to move in this direction.

missing part can stop production, so 1,000 parts sourced from vulnerable locations constitutes a very high degree of risk. It became clear that the company needed better control over its supply chain where key components are concerned (Matsuo, 2015).

In response to these findings, Toyota requested the relevant suppliers either to spread production of their components over more locations, or to hold a safety stock in a location away from the production site. Both of these measures constitute a loss of efficiency, an increase in cost, but an increase also in resilience. In addition, Toyota announced it would design future models with greater commonality of components. This last measure enables suppliers to gain economies of scale such that spreading production over multiple locations may be more viable from an efficiency perspective. In this case, Toyota's supplier associations were able to rally round and organise re-sourcing of key components at short notice, allowing car production to recommence in a matter of weeks (Yuen, 2012). However, this was only possible because in the wake of the worldwide recession, car demand was low and suppliers were mostly working well below capacity – i.e. they had redundancy in the form of spare capacity.

In reality, creating actual redundancy is not always how natural systems work. Species that appear to us as outsiders to play no significant role in the system, and which therefore – to us – appear 'redundant', nevertheless play some role in the system. It is just that in the face of a system change due to an external threat, their role changes into one that may appear to us more prominent. In other words, there is no actual excess capacity in natural systems in the way we understand it. In this way, then, it is more akin to the system suggested recently in the case of Toyota (Fujimoto and Park, 2014). One way of achieving this type of resilience is through investment in equipment with the capability of rapid reprogramming. In this case a software package is retained by the company and when one facility is disrupted, the software can be used to rapidly reprogramme equipment in another plant in order to take over the lost production capacity; this is one example of what has been described as 'virtual dual sourcing' (Fujimoto and Park, 2014). In addition, supplies to the original plant have to be diverted to the new plant, which may now be forced to make a more complex range of products, while such flexible equipment tends to cost more than fixed equipment. However, the fundamental message is that, as in natural systems, in human industrial systems resilience adds cost and is often the converse of efficiency. Yet, in the more recent Kumamoto earthquake of 2016, Toyota was still faced with supply disruptions (Williams, 2016a, 2016b, 2016c), while a fire at a steel supplier and explosion at a brake supplier caused further disruptions, suggesting there are still resilience issues to be addressed (Williams, 2016d, 2016e). The Toyota case illustrates the crucial and continuous trade-off between resilience and efficiency.

18. Supply webs: conclusions

In this chapter and, indeed, in Part III as a whole, an attempt has been made to revisit previous efforts to link business academic thinking with that in ecology in the light, particularly, of advances in the latter, but also in the context of the increasing need for business to engage with the sustainability agenda. In this context, here we focus particularly on SSCM and thereby seek to advance the SSCM agenda on two fronts. First, the need for SSCM theoreticians – and by extension academics in other business disciplines – to consider the extent to which they have long failed to engage with progress in thinking about business and sustainability. In fact, within SSCM it is doubtful such work has contributed significantly to making SCs more sustainable in a scientifically meaningful and measurable sense. The second aspect has been to try and leverage a fuller understanding of sustainability in a business context to encourage SSCM theory to play a leading role in the inevitable transition from a worldview dominated by economic systems to one in tune with ecological thinking. Some suggestions of areas of ecology that could prove useful in this context were briefly explored, building to some extent on the work by Gruner and Power (2017), notably by achieving resilience through understanding the importance of diversity.

If SSCM is able to engage with this ecological agenda, it could be well positioned to play a leading role in the broader transition to a more sustainable economic system, as promoted by more sustainability-aware disciplines and subdisciplines such as industrial ecology, sustainable consumption and production (SCP), de-growth, and others. In the short and medium term there are perhaps more practical implications for SSCM, such as the need to think of the organisation and supply chain as integral parts of ecosystems (Gladwin et al., 1995). It will also require a rethink on a number of other issues, such as the current focus on waste – as waste is not a concept that is relevant from an ecological perspective (waste from one organic process always provides an input for other organic processes) – and also growth and productivity, which are not always in line with a sustainability perspective; i.e. should ecological supply chain management (ESCM) consider issues raised by the

SCP and de-growth literatures? If SSCM were able to make this shift towards what is suggested here could be described as ESCM, could it, by its very nature as a field that permeates many business and economic activities, be a lever to moving a broader set of business disciplines towards greater sustainability? Other issues to consider for integration into such new models include the nature of relationships that are mostly based on a profit-maximising orientation and power seeking, the focus on cost minimisation and that of doing more with less: the search for efficiency. Instead, such a model would highlight concepts and principles from an ecological perspective, which can be applied to reconceptualise the question of resilience in supply chains; concepts such as systemic interdependence and balance, and the notion of scale, both global versus local and also, at the level of the organisation, that of small and larger organisations. In all this it should then aim to replicate the principles of a living system: not a question of resource exploitation but harmonious complementarity and interdependence; a long shot, perhaps, but worthy of further exploration.

PART IV

Are we getting any closer to sustainable consumption, production and supply webs?

19. Solutions?

We start off this part by reviewing a number of approaches that have been proposed to enable the move to a more sustainable economic system. Although all of these can make a contribution, we should also highlight the potential flaws of such approaches in order to avoid the impression that all solutions are already readily available. Particularly in the areas of 'hearts and minds', organisational and social innovation, more work is definitely needed and a way of integrating all these lines of thinking is also overdue – it is still often the case that emphasising one particular problem can lead to problems elsewhere. An example is promoting diesel-engined cars in the EU in order to tackle climate change, while ignoring the local health impacts of this approach at a time when petrol engines were ahead in terms of toxic emissions control technologies. This once again emphasises the need for a systems thinking approach analogous to the way most natural systems operate; that elusive ecological worldview suggested by Krebs (2008).

19.1   CLOSING THE LOOP?

In business sustainability circles much faith is placed in the 'closed loop' (CL) concept, whereby – ideally – no new materials and resources are added to the new 'circular' economy, but those already in the economy are reused and recycled in a perpetual circular process. Although this brief description sketches a simplistic picture, it captures the essence of the concept. This idea has already been embedded in the future economic strategy of a number of countries, while the UK-based Ellen McArthur Foundation has been formed around this very concept and has been actively promoting it. In the context of SCM this gave rise to the sub-field of 'reverse logistics', whereby the supply chain is seen not merely as unidirectional, i.e. from the supplier to the customer, but bi-directional, i.e. also from the market back to the supplier. As an example, to return to our automotive theme, there has long been a system in the car and truck industry whereby an engine at the end of its first phase of useful life is returned for rebuilding and reuse (cf. Steinhilper,

1998). In many cases this is done by independent operators, but it is also often carried out by the original manufacturer, whereby engines rebuilt by the latter command a premium in the market. Often these rebuilt engines are perceived as better, because the stresses inherent in newly cast metal have all been 'ironed' out. For this reason, BMW in the 1980s used the end-of-life blocks of old production car engines in its short-lived Formula 1 programme. In the automotive sector the same has long been the case for transmissions, axles and other major components, while other parts, such as batteries, have long been routinely recycled. These are classic examples of reverse logistics and provide a solid platform for the concept of the closed loop.

In fact, one of the pioneers of the closed loop concept, Walter Stahel (2016) clarified that in his concept of the closed loop economy, extended lifespans and reuse play a central part, something he also explored in earlier work (e.g. Stahel, 1998), and yet 'closed loop' (CL) is often presented in a much simpler form, whereby the current input into the economy remains much as it is today, but at the end of life, products are dismantled and their materials reused for new inputs into the economy. In this form, we are not convinced it represents as significant a contribution to moving to a more sustainable economy as is often suggested; it makes, at best, a partial contribution. Our problems with much of current CL thinking can be summarised as follows:

(1)   CL homes in on levels 2 and 3 of the 'waste hierarchy': *reuse* and *recycle*, while overlooking the first and most important: *reduce*.
(2)   CL implementation carries with it a danger of creating a static system, whereby material innovations are discouraged.
(3)   CL tends to be too vague as to whether the loop should be closed within a single product type (e.g. mobile phones, computers, cars), within one sector (e.g. construction), or within one economy and, if so, is that a local, regional, national economy?

Taking these points one by one, the apparent focus on reuse and recycle could lead to those industries involved in closing the loop becoming dependent on the continuation of the present – excessive – flow of goods and materials through the system for their own survival. If your business model relies on a steady flow of waste plastic, for example, any reduction of that flow – by extending product lifespans, for example – will inevitably have a negative impact on your business, so will be discouraged – understandably – by those lobbying on behalf of that business. The key aim of sustainability, then, of reducing those flows therefore tends to be overlooked or downplayed and yet that is precisely what is needed if we genuinely aim to move towards greater sustainability. There is a danger, therefore, of perpetuating the existing 'failed' system, unless the loop-closing process is seen as part of a more radical transition to a different way of doing things, and that is much more challenging.

Point two is perhaps equally important. Imagine a loop-closing system for the current car business and manufacturing model – as outlined in Part II of this book – predicated on steel bodies, with some plastics and a mixture of cast iron and aluminium mechanical components in known input proportions. We are already seeing the beginnings of a series of new automotive technologies in which the core materials in cars change to more lightweight body–chassis structure materials, such as aluminium (e.g. Jaguar, Tesla Model S), magnesium (e.g. Rolls-Royce), more use of plastics and composites, including carbon fibre (e.g. BMW i3), and a change in powertrain technologies from internal combustion engines to electric traction, leading to new waste streams involving lithium-ion batteries and the novel materials used in those, and in their motors, controllers, etc. There is no doubt that these flows will be dealt with, but the methods needed are different from those for conventional IC cars, thereby not closing the loop. Similarly, if electric vehicle (EV) battery technology now changed from lithium-rich to some other material mix, there may be no demand for the lithium recovered from these now-obsolete technology batteries, and so on. By making businesses and sectors reliant on such specific waste streams, therefore, potential resistance to the introduction of new – and perhaps environmentally more desirable – materials and technologies would be inevitable, putting up unnecessary barriers to their introduction.

Which brings us to point three: should we assume in CL that loops are closed within one product area, or is 'leakage' to other products, sectors, or economies allowed? An assumption of the latter already sees flows of low-value materials – mainly plastics – to less industrialised nations or countries with less enforcement of environmental standards. Even in conventional materials, such as steel ships, we see that recycling does take place but often involves dismantling of ships in dangerous, unhealthy conditions by badly paid labour in poorer countries such as Bangladesh, which is again a reflection of the inherent problems of the globalised 'division of labour' and of whose interests are protected over those of others. Extending product lifespans (Deutsch, 1994; Kostecki, 1998; Cooper, 2005, 2010; Nieuwenhuis, 2008, 2014) would be one way of reducing inputs into the system, but this then also delays the inputs into the loop-closing system, potentially rendering it uncompetitive. It may be possible to build these circular economy firms in such a way that they have the resilience to adapt to different inputs over time, but that does still require a careful balancing of supply and demand. It is possible that, as Dorling (2020) suggests, we are moving into a much more stable period of less frantic change and innovation that will be conducive to building a durable loop-closing system, but it would still need to deal with the legacy of the current transition period in terms of very mixed material flows.

A slightly broader approach was taken by McDonough and Braungart in their influential and inspiring book, *Cradle to Cradle* (2002). Their approach is based more on ecological models and on a system change, whereby they envisage – among other ideas – that all products are designed in such a way that a post-use life is taken into account at the design stage. They seem to see this process much more in terms of natural processes, whereby, for example, wood does not return to a tree after use, but is recycled by fungi and micro-fauna to end up feeding the soil, which then, in turn, provides nutrients for a growing tree (cf. Stamets, 2005). Such more complex 'loops' provide a more realistic model for how future material flows could develop in a more sustainable economic system, provided that system has the necessary resilience and adaptability. It would also have to favour existing materials over new inputs through government action such as regulation or taxation. This is also more like the approach advocated by the academic field of industrial ecology, which promotes the idea of 'eco-industrial parks', whereby companies are co-located, combining those whose processes generate types of waste with companies for which those types of waste are inputs. Although examples are rare, there does seem scope for expanding on this concept. However, here too the points made earlier still apply, in that those firms depending on the waste of their neighbours as inputs into their own processes would also encourage the continuing production of that waste, thereby drawing materials into the system. Although the potential of a completely closed loop may, of course, be there, energy and other resource inputs into the processing cannot be ignored. Human activity on the whole concentrates and refines materials that occur in a dispersed form in natural systems. After use, the natural system then tends to try and disperse those materials again – entropy – which, unfortunately, leaves us with dispersed environmental problems, such as microplastics everywhere.

Finally, as we discuss earlier in the book, abandoning our addiction to endless growth is key here too, but this idea is often missing from the CL debates. Take the example of partnerships between chemistry researchers and businesses proliferating around the advancement of the so-called bio-economy, in particular around the search for new biodegradable materials that could fulfil the post-use life ambitions outlined in *Cradle to Cradle* (2002). This is often seen as a solution with no ecological impact, but does it really have no impact? Despite all best intentions, can we really conceive that discarding of ever-more even completely biodegradable materials will not affect ecosystems? This type of innovation is of course desirable, but as mentioned earlier, it needs to be paired with a much more radical transformation of our production and consumption systems, outside the growth paradigm.

19.2   PRODUCT SERVICE SYSTEMS (PSS)

The closed loop system in its wider sense also promotes the idea of product stewardship, whereby the originator of a product retains respon-sibility for it. This could even be extended to materials stewardship and chemicals leasing, whereby the very materials that make up a product can be leased and recovered at the end-of-life phase to be returned to their owner who then supplies them to a new client. Limited attempts to introduce this into the existing system have been made, but with mixed success. One example is the EU End of Life Vehicle (ELV) Directive, which makes vehicle manufacturers responsible for their products post use and requires 95 per cent of a car's components and materials to be recycled or reused. A laudable initiative, although in practice, end-of-life vehicle take-back is usually handled through third parties and the small cost is merely added to the cost of the new vehicle; no change to the system as such has been achieved, although in reality, much of a car was already recycled in any case and it may have more potential in other sectors.

In order to ensure that the originator of the product does retain a more hands-on responsibility for the product, the product–service system (PSS) has been promoted. Such systems already have a history in some sectors such as commercial printers, photocopiers, lifts in buildings, etc. In many such cases, the end user never owns the hardware, but pays a fee for using the service such machinery provides. When the system fails, it is repaired by the owner, not the user and at the end of its life, the owner replaces the machinery and takes care of its refurbishment or recycling.

In this way, the hardware becomes an asset to the owner's business and any repair or premature disposal becomes a cost to the business, thereby providing an incentive to extend its lifespan. An incentive also exists to make the product such that its lifespan is optimised, as the actual cost of the product does not have to be realised up front, but can be spread over the many years it is in use as a tool for the business to operate with. The longer it can generate income the better, therefore.

It has been suggested that this model could be spread much more widely in consumer goods markets as well. With a product–service system, the product is combined with a service and it is the service that the consumer pays for. In fact, consumer examples of PSS have spread in the past few decades. Many people now lease cars, for example, while car-sharing and bicycle-sharing systems are increasingly common. PSS is seen by many as the most viable future sustainable business model for the reasons outlined. One example of a company promoting this idea is Welsh firm Riversimple, with its small hydrogen fuel-cell car. In their case, the vehicle is allocated to one person, business or family, but in other examples, such as the car-sharing system or 'car club', one car can see many users. With individual users, we could see a core aim as being the extension of a car's lifespan over many years; with current technologies, around 30 years has been suggested as feasible (Porsche, 1976; Nieuwenhuis, 1994). However, with the shared use model, the more intensive use of the vehicle would not necessarily lead to a longer lifespan, but a more intense use of the resources while the vehicle is in use. In either case, refurbishment and upgrading can then provide the product with a second life, to be utilised by new users.

Again, a word of caution with such 'beyond ownership' models. Clearly, where these originate from small idealistic businesses such as Riversimple or grassroots initiatives such as local car-sharing schemes for local communities, they are laudable. However, they could also provide scope for big business to use these as data-gathering and control systems. Again, as with all natural – including human – systems, scale is important in such cases. As with other current developments, such as automated vehicles, the opportunities for such systems to become part of a surveillance capitalism system are ever present (Zuboff, 2019).

20. Is population really a problem?

Speak of human population growth and the iconic figure of Thomas Malthus immediately springs to mind. His 1798 work, *An Essay on the Principles of Population*, became very influential and informed thinking and policymaking in the UK throughout the nineteenth century. In simple terms, he concluded that population growth would only be limited through war and famine and that this was the nature of things. Thus, any attempt to improve the lot of the poor by socio-economic means was doomed to failure and was in fact counterproductive. This concept has been quite persistent, despite much evidence to the contrary, and influenced key economists as well as people like Charles Darwin. More concerning is the fact that, much later, his ideas have often been adopted by environmentalists, who argue that if population could be controlled, there would be sufficient resources for all and we could move towards a more sustainable world. A subtext can often be suspected that, if only there were fewer people in poorer countries, those of us in rich countries could carry on as 'normal'. It is true that the past 200 years or so have seen a massive increase in the human population; in fact, it has been calculated that human biomass is now 100 times that of any other large animal species that has ever lived (Ackerman, 2014, quoting Wilson, 2006).

We want to avoid a detailed review of the literature on population, merely addressing it here as it is such a persistent thread through much environmental writing, and to that extent is relevant to the topics covered here. However, it has become quite clear that as poverty is alleviated and education levels – particularly of women – increase, fertility rates decline and populations stabilise. The problem is therefore not birth rates, but other factors such as income, health care, security and simply the reduction of the need to make sure you have surviving children to look after you in your old age. These factors have all improved over the past 50 years or so. In the light of these findings, the UN has in recent years revised its forecasts for population growth over the current century, now expecting it to peak at around 11 billion at some point later this century, whereafter it is set to decline (UN, 2019). Others, more recently,

have challenged even this estimate (Bricker and Ibbitson, 2019), suggesting a peak at around 8 or 9 billion around the middle of this century.
Dorling (2020) provides a detailed analysis of this trend and by focusing
on changes in the rate of growth, rather than growth as such, places the
points at which the first signs of this decline – in terms of changes in the
rate of growth – set in much earlier than one might expect. For the world
as a whole he is able to place this point in the late 1960s; for China it
was around 1968, well before its one child policy was even introduced;
but for the US, it was much later, in 1997. Even for Africa, the source of
much concern for population watchers, Dorling (2020: 159) shows that
the increase in the rate of growth peaked as early as 1976, while for the
Indian subcontinent it peaked in 1998 (ibid.: 167). Several developed
nations, including Japan, South Korea, Italy and Germany, are now more
concerned about their declining birth rates and aging population.

We generally think of sustainability, and the wider environmental
movement, as a progressive cause – certainly many of those involved
would conceive of themselves in that way. But when a key concern
is overpopulation, we need to face up to the bigoted values that can
underpin it to avoid simply repeating these mistakes. An environmentalism rooted in any manner of inequity is not one worth taking forward.
Thinking about the overpopulation issue, arguments that birth rates
should be curbed will often focus on India or Africa, giving a free pass
to Western countries that have far greater carbon footprints and more
historical responsibility for climate change. Or perhaps the birth rates
under scrutiny are of those on the breadline supported by welfare benefits, perhaps accused of having children to access housing or social security, thus ignoring the larger carbon footprints of the middle class who
purchase (and discard) far more possessions and typically play a larger
role in causing ecological damage through their greater spending power.
Scratch beneath the surface of debates around overpopulation, and the
anxiety that the planet has too many people is an ideological grounding in
eugenics with all the racist, classist and ablest prejudices that accompany
it. The history of environmentalism is writ-through with such prejudice,
the 'scientific racism' – the pseudoscientific beliefs used to justify discrimination – that emerged in the late eighteenth, the nineteenth and early
twentieth centuries, and may still hold some latent sway when discussing
issues of production and consumption.

Founding figures of the modern environmental movement such as
Henry David Thoreau – with his views on First Nations peoples – or John
Muir – and his sentiments towards African Americans – would all offer

illuminating case studies of this trend. Madison Grant, a leading member of the so-called Progressive Era of social and political reform in the United States, though, represents one of the strongest examples of how bigotry can be infused in environmentalism. As Spiro's (2009) account shows, Grant has been labelled both the 'nation's most influential racist' and the 'greatest conservationist that ever lived'. That both labels could be applied to the same figure does more than speak to the typical cop-out used when defending such figures, that these were different times. Rather, it reflects a prominent figure fighting to establish these views as mainstream, both in wider society and, more specifically, within the environmental movement.

Grant was a key figure in establishing the wildlife management movement and is credited with helping to save many species from extinction. He helped to establish the Bronx Zoo as well as founding the first organisations dedicated to preserving American bison and the Californian redwoods. He was also author of *The Passing of the Great Race*, a 1916 work charting the racial history of Europe and expressing concerns about the changing 'stock' of American immigration of the early twentieth century. Adolf Hitler called the book his 'bible' in a letter to Grant, while it underpinned the Immigration Act 1924, which banned immigration from Asia to the United States. Grant's environmentalism and his eugenics went hand-in-hand as can be found in Purdy's (2019) account of his work. He saw a need for careful stewardship and management of the species he loved. Natural resources needed to be conserved for the 'Nordic' race that he saw as a natural aristocracy, noble and with an instinct for political governance. He was happier in nature, in part because it allowed him to escape a society that he saw as increasingly full of base, unworthy humanity. He bemoaned modern, industrial society for violating the laws of 'survival of the fittest' both by allowing what he viewed as inferior specimens to thrive through the provision of welfare to the poor by the state, and by destroying 'the fittest', such as by clear-felling forests indiscriminately. Grant believed that his generation had 'the responsibility of saying what forms of life shall be preserved'. Thinking of 'nature' as excluding people is one of the key problems of our society, something we have already addressed. We have to see ourselves as an integral part of natural systems in order to move forward. Botkin (2017) rightly highlights the notion that 'People are outside of nature' as one of his '25 Myths that Are Destroying the Environment', the title of his book.

Grant is not especially well remembered in the environmental movement today, but he was well-connected, hugely admired and, crucially, influential – with the ear of presidents such as Teddy Roosevelt – and he has an important legacy in foregrounding respect for non-human life over that of fellow human beings deemed less worthy. Nature was a refuge from accepting the rise of people he felt challenged by. This is a process that, following Said (1978), we can label 'orientalism'; the patronising and demeaning construction of a less civilised other. We can see similar today in debates centred on the idea that this nature needs to be protected from some of humanity; and the way that the eugenics legacy in population debates tends to mean protecting from the poor, non-white and Global South.

While Grant has been all but forgotten, more celebrated figures in environmentalism still carry such baggage. Garrett Hardin's (1968) article, 'The tragedy of the commons', still holds an important place in modern environmentalism; originally published in *Science*, it is frequently republished, widely cited and forms a part of many a university syllabus in environmental science and beyond. Hardin focuses on human population growth and the use of the Earth's natural resources. He begins with a history of the English commons –collectively owned and managed land – and uses this as the basis for his key claim that the commons were undermined by human selfishness. He identifies an impulse for people to overgraze their livestock on such public land.

Hardin uses this set-up for a wider critique of governance that he believes privileges the undeserving and feckless, and which in time will bring society to ruin. State support, in his neo-Malthusian analysis, leads to overbreeding and should be cut. State support, of course, is provided to the poorest members of society so, in allowing them to breed, Hardin sees the roots of the crisis. This is his tragedy. He criticises the welfare state. In a section headed 'Freedom to breed is intolerable', Hardin (1968: 1246) states that, 'if each human family were dependent only on its own resources; if the children of improvident parents starved to death; if, thus, overbreeding brought its own "punishment" to the germ line then there would be no public interest in controlling the breeding of families'. The reason that children are not allowed to starve to death, which he regrets, is the existence of the welfare state.

Hardin also targeted the Universal Declaration of Human Rights in a similar vein. In describing the family as the natural and fundamental unit of society under Article 16, he was concerned by the notion that decisions on whether and what size family to have rested with the families themselves. For Hardin (1968: 1246), 'if we love the truth we must openly deny the validity of the Universal Declaration of Human Rights, even though it is promoted by the United Nations'. His concerns on allowing choice are clear when Hardin (1968: 1246) questions, 'how shall we deal with the family, the religion, the race, or the class (or indeed any distinguishable and cohesive group) that adopts overbreeding as a policy to secure its own aggrandizement'. The Southern Poverty Law Centre lists Hardin as a White Nationalist for his bigoted rhetoric. He served on the board of directors of the anti-immigrant Federation for American Immigration Reform as well as the nativist Social Contract Press. His link between environmentalism and eugenics cannot be dismissed as a relic, for he published into the 1990s, and a foundation currently works in his name to promote the ongoing influence of his work on the environmental movement.

For overpopulation, read over-production and over-consumption. Common arguments in environmentalism over the last few decades run the line of 'if everyone in the world consumed the same as the average North American' then we are all doomed. For Benton (2002: 84), 'it is a short jump from this to the assertion that environmentalism is a Western, if not white middle-class social movement, the main objective of which is to prevent developing countries from doing what those in the West have already done'. While such arguments might have an element of self-criticism and reflexivity to them, they also hold an implicit threat and a warning that others should not aspire to such standards and that we need to act now before they get ideas above their station. It shifts blame to emerging markets in the Global South or those struggling but desiring more at home. Having secured the good life for ourselves, we now want to keep it to ourselves by pulling up the drawbridge in the name of environmental concerns. What we see is the bigoted self-interest of a white, Western middle class to preserve its own values and protect its own lifestyle at the expense of the poor and underprivileged.

So, when population is made a problem, it is too often a case of: whose population? And when what people are buying, or eating or using is queried, it can sadly be a question of: who is buying, eating and using? There are judgements made about those who are entitled and those who should fall in line and go without. Perhaps, this is part of the reason that Carter (2018) can talk about how environmental groups have been overwhelmingly white and middle class. He identifies the manner in which this homogeneity has led to a specific understanding of sustainability through a Western, white and middle-class lens that holds us back from the more holistic environmentalism that is needed to properly deal with the problems we face.

Agyeman et al. (2002: 5) suggest an approach to sustainability that addresses 'the need to ensure a better quality of life for all, now and into the future, in a just and equitable manner, whilst living within the limits of supporting ecosystems'. Such an approach prioritises justice and equity without downplaying the environment as the ecosystem that sustains us. Agyeman (2008) highlights how much existing theorising and activity on sustainability are based on environmental stewardship and rooted in the New Environmental Paradigm of Catton and Dunlap (1978). For Agyeman (2008: 752), 'such approaches may be very good on "inter-generational equity" – equity to as yet unborn generations – but ha[ve] little to say about "intra-generational equity" – equity or social justice now'. This gap, which even the Brundtland Report (WCED, 1987) addressed, is what he labels as the 'equity deficit' of environmental sustainability. We need to proceed aware also of the intersecting inequalities that cut across societies around the world. For example, we have talked about food in this book. We must pay attention to the way race and class play a role in production and consumption of food, which Alkon and Agyeman (2011) demonstrate to be sometimes absent from the mainstream food movement narrative. Instead, food justice projects can work to empower local communities to grow, sell and eat food that is fresh, local and sustainable but, crucially, culturally appropriate and produced with respect for the local land and the people. Another topic we have considered at length is the motor vehicle. Newman (2017) has written on how current trends for remodelling the car system largely involve the substitution of petrol/diesel for potentially more ecologically sound methods of powering the vehicles, such as electricity, which simply acts to exacerbate mobility related exclusion. Those who cannot afford to buy a new car or those who, for example, through ill-health are not able to operate their own vehicle, can be cut off from society – no matter how much more virtuously green it feels – which necessitates the creation of a Mobility Bill of Rights that moves beyond considering the environment in isolation.

What we are proposing in this book is for a sustainability approach that will avoid shifting blame onto those pining for the consumer lifestyles they have been taught are aspirational. We do not want to advocate one rule for one and one for another. We do not see any one group as more deserving of access to the stuff that they want. The wrong turn has been made in the total abandon to a capitalist system premised upon rampant, unrelenting accumulation. Dorling (2020: 231) argues that this too represents a transitory phase in human development:

> Capitalism is a transition. It is not a mode of production. A mode implies a degree of stability. There has been no stability under capitalism (or the communist reactions to it) – neither demographic, economic, nor social. Capitalism is a period of change from social systems that were stable ... to something else that we have not yet reached, which will probably also be stable.

In this book we aim to provide some suggestions of aspects of this future stable system. Encouraging us all to look towards taking on less but better stuff – things that will last with us over the life course, which we will cherish and that are truly worthy of taking on as part of our identities – is a small way forward for all. It is a bunch of middle-class Europeans telling every one of us to make a sacrifice for us, it is promoting a new way of relating to the objects that surround us and a reformed economic system based on this principle. For any such developments to occur in a world still structured by a capitalism that has racist, classist, and gendered discrimination deeply ingrained is, of course, optimistic. We are not saying it would be easy or a simple transition. But we are suggesting it is an alternative that should be considered by those who care about sustainability and are committed to pushing through change that can benefit everyone on the planet. We think this has a potential to be a fairer, more equitable transition to sustainability – one that means more people have a prospect of living the lives they want to live, all while causing less environmental damage; and it is not as if it has never been tried anywhere before.

21. Will innovation save us?

In conventional economics there is a strong strand of thinking that technological innovation will solve most of our problems, something we have touched upon in our discussion of growth/degrowth. For the ecological problems facing us, this has also often been suggested. Of course, if this works, we do need to put the necessary resources into such priorities, otherwise those innovations will not happen. Here, the role of the public sector has been overlooked in recent decades as the private sector has come to be seen as more innovative and more efficient. We explored the efficiency concept earlier, especially in Part III, while Mazzucato (2013, 2019) has highlighted the key role of the public sector in the development of the pre-market technologies needed for that private sector innovation to even happen. But what of the prospects of innovating ourselves out of the current problems? Apart from the fact that many solutions to our problems are already available and merely need to be applied, Dorling (2020) in his analysis of rates of growth also discovered that the rate of technological innovation has been slowing down. We have become used to the rate of innovation of the nineteenth and twentieth centuries and have come to think of it as normal. However, as Dorling points out (2020: 85–87) this may well have been a temporary phase and we may be returning to the slower rates of innovation of previous centuries, although these are probably more like those of the Middle Ages (Gimpel, 1976) than of the Palaeolithic. The much-vaunted Moore's 1965 law of processor power seems to be grinding to a halt after some 50 years, although this reflects a history of around 70–80 years of technology development. In this context, for example, the latest iPhone's main innovation seems to constitute the software behind its camera, which, while admittedly very clever, is an enhancement of existing technology.

The ICT industry often argued that if the car industry was as innovative as the ICT sector we would have flying cars by now. Safety concerns, manufacturing issues – such as those explored in Part II – and practicalities such as the ability to be used in different driving environments from −50 to +50 degrees C limit what one can do with cars. Also, much innovation in cars took place in the first 70–80 years after Daimler and Benz. In fact, that takes us to the 1960s and cars from that era are still perfectly usable today, showing how limited real progress since then has indeed been. Within automotive, the major revolution at present is the shift from internal combustion (IC) to electric vehicles (EV), in other words, drawing on a basic technology that was pioneered in the 1840s (EV) and 1860s (rechargeable batteries), before petrol and diesel engines even appeared.

Innovations now include applications of existing technologies to new areas such as automated cars, although here, again, ICT is meeting the real-world barriers that the car industry has long been used to. Not surprising, therefore, that the main proponents of this range of technologies are in the ICT industry and not the car industry. Not only does this – to many unnecessary technology (Wolmar, 2018) – turn out to be more difficult to implement in real-world driving conditions than its proponents expected, with current energy needs, the processing power required for automated driving would demand some 40 per cent of the energy carried on board an EV, although greater efficiencies will no doubt be achieved over time. Of course, a human driver can do all this on a bowl of cereal or rice. We should also remember that 'artificial intelligence' (AI) is, in reality, merely enhanced human intelligence, something humans probably do better, although AI does it faster once it has received that basic human input. In addition, concerns have been raised about the new materials that need to be accessed (see also Chapter 19, Section 19.1, in respect of the circular economy) as well as the data collected by such systems and how this would be used, providing the ability to track people's travel in some detail (Zuboff, 2019). In the foreseeable future, automated vehicles will therefore mainly find application in carefully controlled environments with known and predictable hazards, such as certain urban and suburban areas in industrialised countries.

Nevertheless, it is clear that these trends will lead to significant change. Energy for an EV can be generated from renewables, while over time other energy needs, such as home heating and cooling, could also be delivered this way. Such developments would phase out some major concerns of the existing sustainability model, notably to begin to address both climate change and local air quality. EVs also bring the ability for localised power generation and supply through, for example, wind generators and solar panels, making rural areas players in the energy supply sector and ideally suited to EVs (Nieuwenhuis, 2018b). This would rapidly make the oil industry obsolete, thereby tackling another major concern of current sustainability thinking, while changing the balance in international relations: control over oil or gas would no longer equate to political or diplomatic power. At the same time, energy supply could be decentralised into local communities. These changes already underway will change the fundamentals of our economies in quite significant ways. On the other hand, new materials need to be accessed, explored and developed in order to support these technologies. Only once sufficient material exists within our system, and a stable set of technologies has been found, could a closed loop economy then help to reduce the need for new inputs of raw materials, even if energy is all renewable by that stage. It is clear, therefore, that current technology trends do have the potential of dealing with many of our concerns in the context of sustainability, provided the required resources are put in place to keep the existing momentum going. All this is not going to be cheap, and will cost jobs in legacy industries, but will also generate new opportunities in the newly emerging sectors and services brought into being by these changes. Supply webs could change dramatically as a result. However, would this also deal with over-consumption and over-production? Or would these matter less if their environmental impacts are reduced? However, before we become too relaxed, climate change will continue for a few centuries yet, just from what we have already put into the system over the past few centuries, or even millennia, since agriculture started (Ruddiman, 2005). Also, none of this addresses the plastics and other toxic chemicals already in the environment and still being dumped into the environment, nor the ongoing extinction of species, many of which we are not even aware of, and while congested streets full of EVs may be cleaner, they are still congested.

In addition to technological innovations, we should therefore also be thinking about the social innovations needed. Sperling (2018) argues that automated vehicles will only work if they are also electrified and shared. Individual ownership of automated vehicles would lead to abuse, he argues. Examples would include commuting to work, then sending the car home to park itself to avoid high parking charges downtown, or sending the car out to pick up a pizza. Such – natural for humans – abuses would increase congestion, resource use, etc. Shared use, by contrast, would instil a degree of control and discipline to the use of such vehicles. In short, automated vehicles are more likely to develop into a new, additional mode and as such are unlikely to replace the privately owned car, or the vehicle for personal use, such as in a product–service system (PSS) model, although demand for these could decline dramatically. Speaking of PSS models, as mentioned, scale matters; where such systems hand over control and data collection to governments or large corporations, data security and privacy concerns inevitably arise (Zuboff, 2019), while if these are retained within small, local firms, collectives or co-operatives, control can be retained within the local community or by the individual. Social innovations extend well beyond vehicles, of course, although they are becoming symbolic and indicative of the thinking among 'tech' companies; as Crawford (2020: 7) points out: 'The boosters of driverless cars are unimpressed with pleasure as an ideal and suspicious of individual judgement', as they would prefer to do the judgement for us. More on this later. One of the possible outcomes of the Covid-19 crisis, raging as we finalise this book, is the likelihood of more people working from home. Such a move could in itself have social and environmental benefits, including less travel, reduced congestion and energy use, lower stress levels, etc. It also means that businesses predicated on people travelling to and being at a centralised placed of work will suffer, including businesses involved in making, selling and repairing cars, those providing public transport, and some catering facilities. At the same time, demand for ICT will increase, as will demand for local coffee shops and similar facilities where home workers spend time to avoid isolation at home. All this only applies to some occupations, of course. Manufacturing workers will need to be where the investments in their production processes have been made, while supply chains still need logistics workers to move items. And yet, here too, we could see greater localisation and decentralisation towards smaller-scale facilities operating smarter, lower-fixed-cost manufacturing systems closer to their workforce and customers.

22. Alternatives to mass production

Other promising areas of innovation involve improved manufacturing technologies, such as 3D printing. These are now finding a role in more mainstream applications, including in automotive (Lutz, 2020), which could well enable that transition away from mass production. As outlined earlier, according to Sabel and Zeitlin (1985, 1997), mass production was not an inevitable outcome of developments in the early twentieth century. Alternatives were and could have been equally viable, as is evidenced by the survival of a number of low-volume specialist car manufacturers, using a range of technologies to produce their chassis, bodies and – in some cases – engines. Eighty years or so on, one option seemed to be abandoning the all-steel body by revisiting some of these alternatives and possibly adopting different car manufacturing technologies. These new technologies were normally reserved for low-volume, high-end cars such as Ferrari, Aston Martin, Rolls-Royce, or the French producers of 'grandes routières' described in Part II, makers of micro-cars (also known as quadricycles or 'voitures sans permis' (VSP)) mainly in France, as well as heavy trucks and buses. The idea was then to combine these characteristics of low-volume vehicle production with more of the retail, distribution and aftermarket activities, which often appeared to be more profitable than purely making and selling cars.

The micro-factory retailing (MFR) model proposed in Wells and Nieuwenhuis (2000), Nieuwenhuis and Wells (2003, 2009) and Nieuwenhuis (2018a) highlights such an alternative business and manufacturing model. The advantages of MFR are several. First of all, the abandoning of Budd all-steel body technology avoids the very high investments in capital equipment needed for this (press shop, press tools, body-in-white, and paint). Although this step also means abandoning high-volume production, it does allow for a dispersed network of local assembly facilities. This network could be rooted in local communities, and cater for local tastes and needs, but could benefit from economies of scale in components and subassemblies such as powertrain, which could be shared by a number of notionally competing manufacturers. This idea is much like the way mountain bikes are made and marketed, providing a template for a useful alternative business model. Ironically, as mentioned earlier, Ford often used a not dissimilar approach for the Model T, which – consisting as it did of a set of mechanical components, but no body – was often shipped to local markets as a kit for local assembly and for locally made bodies to be fitted.

The potential viability of such models is shown by the fact that some low-volume manufacturers already use elements of such a business model. In this context, the UK in particular provides helpful examples, as firms like the Morgan Motor Company and Lotus are of particular interest. Contrary to popular belief, their products – despite being built in much lower numbers – are no more expensive than their mass-produced or volume-produced competitors. In essence, they have offset high capital investment against higher investment in skilled labour. The only penalty is an inability to produce at higher volumes, but also the absence of any need to produce in high volumes to recoup their investment costs. Herein lies the core of a new business model. The Morgan Motor Company's business model relies on making low volumes of durable cars tailored to the requirements of individual customers (Nieuwenhuis and Katsifou, 2015). In a world increasingly in need of sustainable consumption and production, this business model makes increasing sense. This is despite the fact that Morgan's business model dates back over 100 years.

About 70–80 million cars are produced worldwide each year, a practice that is clearly unsustainable. In the longer term, if car-making is to survive, then all car manufacturers will have to move towards a business model closer to that of low-volume manufacturers. Lower volumes would be produced, but the business would survive by helping keep the cars on the road after the initial sale, extending the life of the automobile. Morgan itself produces fewer than 1,500 cars a year, and can be regarded as using a partial version of micro-factory retailing, or MFR (Wells and Nieuwenhuis, 2000; Nieuwenhuis and Wells, 2003, 2009; Nieuwenhuis, 2018a). The MFR business model offers a number of key advantages over Ford–Budd style mass production. These advantages make it inherently more sustainable in economic, social and environmental terms. Investments in productive capacity – a micro factory could typically have a capacity of around 5,000 units a year – are incremental, expandable in line with market demand. Surplus demand is managed through waiting lists – a process often used by Morgan. This situation also ensures continuity of both production and employment.

One crucial advantage of MFR is that capacity can be expanded in discreet increments as small-scale manufacturing units are added. This results from the fact that with much lower capital investments per unit, much smaller production units are viable. The incremental expansion of capacity means that new plants can be added to develop new markets, while new products or variants can be introduced incrementally, resulting in risk reduction. In addition, customers can be shown around the plant and meet the people who make their car and can thereby feel 'closer' to the product. This has long been a feature of the Morgan approach, and is even used by more mainstream volume car-makers trying to build brand loyalty: including Mercedes-Benz, VW, Porsche, and BMW.

Under the MFR model, the factory does not only produce the car – which would still make it dependent on 'moving the metal' – but it adds downstream activities that already tend to be more profitable than building mass-produced cars, as it becomes the location for repair, spare parts, upgrading, restoration and modification. This allows the manufacturer to tap into the elusive but potentially very profitable aftermarket revenue stream, while regular updating and upgrading allows the car to 'grow' with its owner, thereby enhancing retention and vehicle lifespans for greater sustainability; something Tesla is already exploring with its regular 'over the air' software updates. Thus, the factory can undergo a transition over time from an essentially new car production focus, to one more involved in service and repair; then the factory does not depend solely on the sale of new cars. Another UK small-volume producer, Bristol Cars, exploited this model well (Parsons, 2002; Balfour, 2009).

The inherent flexibility of small-scale manufacturing provides better customer care, as well as shorter lead times, and late configuration. In addition, this model builds stronger worker commitment to the product and to customers. This results in more satisfying work for staff, and is likely to result in better quality levels with all the benefits this entails. It also builds higher skill levels in local communities as people are trained locally in these technologies. This manufacturing approach also builds new supply networks as it can take advantage of local small-scale suppliers adding content appreciated by local markets and adding more local jobs. At the same time, modular supply strategies combined with commodity or off-the-shelf purchasing can reduce cost and achieve economies of scale where these are most appropriate, such as in power-train – and with the advent of electric vehicles, this increasingly includes batteries, controllers and electric traction motors.

Abandoning the integral or monocoque body for more modular construction allows quick and easy product upgrades. Thus, technologies that meet the latest environmental and safety standards can often be retrofitted – a major area of obsolescence in the current system – while the vehicle can also be tailored to changing customer needs and wants; even interiors, for example, could be designed to be easily changed and upgraded over time. Small-scale manufacturing processes have a lower environmental impact compared with traditional high-volume manufacturing (Schumacher, 1973). These facilities would involve medium-scale industrial units, whereas a modern car plant occupies several square kilometres of land. Compared with this, Morgan operates from a classic 'light industrial' facility. MFR facilities meet social and political objectives by creating local employment in high-value manufacturing activities. At a time when mass-production jobs are being globalised, the MFR approach makes a key contribution in retaining those skills and adding value within the local market. The MFR facility does not necessarily sell the car, but would be equally viable as manager of a product–service system, whereby it would own the car and sell a mobility service to the user under a leasing-style arrangement, as proposed by Welsh hydrogen fuel-cell car company Riversimple. Riversimple is advocating a product–service system (PSS) approach as part of its business model. They have enhanced the MFR concept by adding a novel governance approach that includes a body of six 'custodians' who represent different stakeholders, such as the environment, customers, the local community, staff, investors and commercial partners/suppliers. These act as an independent body guiding the business. Riversimple argues this allows them to 'see in all directions' (Riversimple, 2017).

Mass production and, specifically, the technologies adopted to enable it, are the key problem in moving the supply side, at least, on to a more sustainable footing (Nieuwenhuis and Wells, 1997, 2003). In this context, it is interesting to review – in addition to these recent examples – some earlier alternatives to the mass production system developed in response to its growth. For example, in the French coach-built luxury car sector, whose demise was outlined earlier, one coachbuilder, Faget-Varnet, patented a new intermediate technology approach. Abandoning wood-frame construction, they developed a basic steel substructure that could be fitted to a chassis and onto which could then be fitted a range of different body styles (Colin, 2003: 94–97). These subframes were welded together from simple folded steel panels to form a stiff structure ready to receive external panels to create a coupé or convertible body as part of a low-cost, low-investment, flexible all-steel structure. Other, more recent, examples include the earlier generations of the Renault Espace, developed by Matra in France as a galvanised steel space-frame to which composite panels could be attached, or the Fiat Multipla of the 1990s, made of simple, low-tooling-cost modular steel structures (Nieuwenhuis and Wells, 1997). Another interesting example of an intermediate, lower-volume response to the Budd–Ford system was Facel Vega in France, as outlined earlier.

22.1   IMPACT OF MFR

A number of firms have already adopted elements of this potentially more sustainable system, while others used it to justify their existing working practices with potential investors. These firms include Morgan Motor Co., Gordon Murray Design – whose 'iStream' manufacturing model was inspired by MFR, Welsh hydrogen car developer Riversimple and American open-source car design company Local Motors. Local Motors enhanced the model by recruiting potential buyers as product developers on an open-source design basis. It also pioneered the use of additive manufacturing, or 3D printing, in this context and has in fact adopted the term 'microfactories' for their dispersed network of facilities.[1] Such contact with industry has allowed the refining of aspects of the model over the intervening years (e.g. Wells and Orsato, 2005; Wells, 2013; Nieuwenhuis, 2014; Nieuwenhuis and Katsifou, 2015). Thinking in terms of alternatives to mass production is still challenging for many in the industry, as well as in academia. Thus, Holweg and Pil (2004: 194) challenged the MFR idea as presented in Wells and Nieuwenhuis (2000), although more recent academic work tends to be more positive towards the feasibility of distributed manufacturing models, at least in the longer term. Holmström et al. (2016), for example, recognise the inevitable outcome of developments such as additive manufacturing on future manufacturing models. There are other socio-economic industrial evolutions, such as other more decentralising trends in the economy: distributed electricity generation through small, dispersed wind farms, solar panels on house roofs, as well as trends towards smaller manufacturing units in a range of industries including tyres, steel and brewing (Wells, 2013). In this respect, then, although Holmström et al. (2016) present their paper as merely setting a future research agenda in this area, the MFR concept appears to be gaining increasing credibility, even in academia.

Given this alternative model, the case of Tesla is very interesting. Hailed very much as a 'future' car company, in manufacturing terms it is still surprisingly similar to 'legacy' car companies. Tesla's innovation lies in its battery-electric drive train technology, its use of interior space to capitalise on the different vehicle layout an EV powertrain allows, increasingly on its growing understanding of how vehicle structures and manufacturing can be simplified as a result of moving to an EV powertrain, but also in its highly vertically integrated business model. Tesla controls not only the production of the powertrain and vehicle structure, but also of key components and subassemblies like batteries, even though it does this with partners. However, through its solar panel subsidiary, Solar City, its Powerwall domestic battery technology and its charger network, it is also involved in the energy supply for its vehicles (see Figure 15.1). This would be like a car company also being involved in petrol and diesel supply as oil extractors, refiners and distributors. Although there was something of this in the early days of the motor car, this model has now disappeared. In addition, Tesla owns its own distribution and service network, something that is rare, though not unheard of in traditional car companies, although where the latter do own dealerships, as with Toyota in Japan, Mercedes in Germany or Renault in France, they operate above or alongside independent private operators. Not so with Tesla, where all sales and service staff are, effectively, Tesla employees. The regular online communication with the vehicles already in the market and the ongoing software updates that this enables are also a major novelty in automotive terms.

And yet, Tesla is setting up a 'Buddist' mass production system very similar to what we have seen in the conventional industry for the past 100 years or so. Although, at present, this allows the supply of its cars at the still growing level of demand, it is unclear what the plan is for when that demand is satisfied. A century ago, car companies that reached that point started marketing efforts – something Tesla has so far avoided – and regular model renewal. The mass production system, as we have seen in Part II, depends on constant supply and therefore needs constant demand. Tesla's model range of models S, 3, X, and Y (meant to spell 'sexy' by the way), seems a credible product offering and these cars have the potential to last a long time. Tesla's introduction of a '1 million mile' battery further emphasises the durability aspect of the cars. In any case, its claims of environmental high ground would become severely compromised if premature disposal of these very resource-intensive cars were to be encouraged merely to stimulate demand for new Teslas. In this context, one wonders how sustainable the current manufacturing approach is, even if other aspects of its business model do have the potential of a more sustainable model, particularly keeping repair, maintenance and used car sales within the Tesla network.

As outlined in Part II, one of the flaws of Ford's approach when it moved to mass production in 1908 and then to the moving production line in 1914 was that it did so with an 'Edwardian' concept of what a car was, thereby missing out on the major body technology change under development at the same time at Budd. You wonder whether Tesla, by adopting the established automotive mass production model from the old 'regime' will also come unstuck once market saturation has been achieved. Although its current manufacturing approach at least involves building factories near the main Tesla markets – California for most models, Texas for the CBRTRK (both for North America), Berlin for European markets and Shanghai for the Far East – the total capacity that is thus being built may prove excessive once markets for Teslas are saturated and its network increasingly emphasises keeping the existing cars on the road. If that is not the case, Tesla will merely perpetuate the existing unsustainable automotive system with its mass production push system and thereby support the unsustainable economic growth model. In this respect, firms such as Riversimple seem more future-proof in their business model, despite their lack of resources.

22.2 CONCLUSIONS: FUTURE MANUFACTURING

In conclusion, in any future sustainable automotive ecosystem, therefore, a version of micro-factory retailing could become one of the dominant business models for the supply and use of motorised personal mobility. MFR would be based on networks of small, dispersed, combined assembly, retail and aftercare or lifetime management (e.g. maintenance and repair, parts supply, upgrade, vehicle management and takeback) facilities that could operate car use under a product–service system (PSS), whereby ownership is retained by the company and users pay for their use. Alternatively, cars could still be sold, but repair and maintenance retained by the MFR, who would also take the vehicle back at the end of its use phase and refurbish it for the next customer. This business model would supply local markets, sourcing from local suppliers, while being rooted in local economies and in tune with local needs. MFRs would also source standardised modules globally from larger, more centralised facilities, which would be able to achieve economies of scale in modules such as structural assemblies, batteries, controllers and powertrains. This process could entail some transport over longer distances, although this would involve smaller subassemblies and modules, rather than complete cars. In fact, it could easily be applied not just to private cars, but also to dedicated shared car-club cars (e.g. Autolib's Bluecar), automated vehicles, dedicated taxis, or public transport modes such as buses, or commercial vans, all adapted to local conditions.

The cost of transport and supply chain complexity for shared mass-produced components and subassemblies would have to be offset by the advantages of economies of scale. It is conceivable for some of the mass car manufacturers in the current mass production industry to become module suppliers in such an alternative model. It is even conceivable that some of these mass producers become MFRs themselves, or spin off existing specialist MFR-like operations to become their core activities (Nieuwenhuis and Wells, 2003), although the precise nature of the product would also have to change to more environmentally optimised vehicles (Nieuwenhuis and Wells, 1997: Chapter 7). Moreover, in a PSS the actual cost of the product is less important, as this can be recovered over several leases over many years – durability and upgradability become key criteria; the need for a 'cheap' car is therefore much reduced, making expensive new technologies more viable, as is suggested by the Riversimple business model (Riversimple, 2017).

One of MFR's main distinguishing features in relation to the current mass production system is that it would break through the 'monoculture' of large centralised factories making a standardised, relatively undifferentiated product in very large numbers and at relatively low cost. Low cost and manufacturing-push make these cars effectively disposable, with short useful lifespans of only 10–15 years. These large facilities draw on complex global supply networks and supply global markets. They may be compared with the farms of the wheat-belt of the US and Canadian prairies in that they too are monoculture-based, supply world markets with cheap standardised grain and draw in supplies – in the form of oil-based pesticides, herbicides and fertilisers – along global supply lines. This model too is now considered by an increasing number of observers to be ultimately unsustainable (Benyus, 1997; Diamond, 2005). Jeffries (1997: 5) gives the example of the monoculture of potatoes in Ireland in the 1840s and the resulting famine as an example of the negative consequences of such an approach in agriculture.

The change process from mass production to MFR is difficult to predict, however, as system change may happen suddenly after a long period of apparent stability (Walker and Salt, 2006; Perrings, 1998). It is also important to note that as the existing system becomes less able to fulfil the needs of the market or the economy in the broadest sense, change becomes inevitable and it is quite possible that the '3 Revolutions' (Sperling, 2018) could be the trigger for such change. As Perrings (1998: 506) observes:

> The economic value of a system in some state depends on its ability to maintain the flow of goods and services for which it is valued given the shocks or disturbances it faces. The source of disturbances may be either anthropogenic or 'natural'.

In our context we could see these disturbances as being generated by the dual forces of market pressure and the need for greater sustainability. Peterson (2000) discusses a model for ecosystem change first proposed by Holling (1986) and developed further in Gunderson et al. (1995). Their cycle moves through rapid growth, conservation, collapse and reorganisation. In the stable phase – the Ford–Budd automotive system during the 1950s and 1960s for example – the system becomes increasingly dependent on the persistence of its existing structure. This makes it vulnerable to anything that might upset it by releasing its organised capital. This kind of system is increasingly stable, but, Peterson (2000) argues, over a decreasing range of conditions and this therefore reduces the resilience of the system. In this respect, then, as the current system has largely favoured efficiency over resilience (Walker and Salt, 2006) it may ultimately not need a massive shock to prompt its transition to an alternative system. The latter may well involve something along the lines of the MFR business model, in view of its greater inherent sustainability in social, environmental, but also ultimately, economic terms.

NOTES

1. https://localmotors.com/microfactories/.

23. Conclusions: SCP and SSCM – an elusive vision?

Well, here we are, reaching the final chapter in this book. We have tried – for the first time we believe – to tackle the problems inherent in our current economic model, as exemplified by its unsustainable consumption patterns, in an integrated manner, recognising that it is driven by unsustainable production systems and business models, while being facilitated by unsustainable supply chains. Having explored these notions, some possible ways forward have also emerged, although we would by no means claim to have found a cast-iron solution to any of these problems. We have tried to summarise some of the possible ways forward that have emerged in Figures 23.1a and 23.1b, although this is clearly not comprehensive; merely a few initial foundation stones for an alternative model have emerged from our work. More than ever, the phrase 'more research needed' is apt here, but we should add that in many cases, solutions are already available – some examples are outlined in this part of the book – and merely require implementation, although that is in itself never easy. In addition, it is increasingly evident that the 2020 coronavirus, Covid-19 or SARSCov2 crisis could have long-term consequences that may make people question our global connectedness, perhaps increasingly favouring the local, but also the whole way we work, consume and produce. At the time of writing it is too early to tell.

We hope also that we have been able to demonstrate that most of the responsibility for our current unsustainable over-consumption in industrialised countries is, in fact, the responsibility of the supply side, industry, business, and especially large corporations which – as is illustrated by our detailed case study of the car industry – needed to develop mass markets for the products that could now be mass produced, but that also *had* to be mass produced in order to meet the needs of the new economies of scale that came with the mass production technologies adopted. This fact is often lost in the academic – and consumer – literature that has long chosen the consumer, rather than the producer, as its primary focus and allocated primary responsibility accordingly. Furthermore, that crucial link between production and consumption, the supply chain (or web) hardly ever features in much of the literature. Analyses of unsustainable consumption have therefore often presented a partial picture of the problem, often making any proposed solutions meaningless.

This problem of producer-led consumption has now entered a new phase with the rise of the so-called 'tech' companies (as if other companies don't do technology), which seek a much more intensive, all-encompassing control of markets and consumers to a degree older companies could only dream of. These are taking even more control away from consumers and citizens through initiatives like autonomous cars, innovations like satellite navigation, permanent location tracking, etc. Although often useful and adding value for people, nevertheless, firms like Google, Amazon, Facebook, Apple and Alibaba seek a new level of control. Yet, on the positive side, firms like eBay have also provided platforms that have enabled small businesses to access world markets, thus benefitting local communities – albeit often at a price – while a new exchange of pre-owned goods among consumers and small businesses has helped extend the lifespan of many consumer goods and industrial goods, providing them with a second or third life when otherwise they could have ended up in landfill. Despite some of these positive aspects, this new wave of consumption, production (including of services) and supply requires more careful monitoring, consideration and public debate than it currently enjoys. We have already seen that such firms – firmly believing they are 'the good guys' – are perfectly prepared to interfere in our democratic systems. As Crawford (2020: 22) points out in the context of the 'tech' firms' keenness on automated cars:

> A passenger is detached, isolated from others, whereas the give-and-take of urban driving is a realm of interaction that demands the skills of cooperation and improvisation. As such, driving is a form of organic civic life ... Driving is a way of interacting with others while having shared, concrete interests at stake. Alexis de Tocqueville suggested that the habits of collective self-government are cultivated in practical activities like this that demand cooperation, and such habits are indispensable to democratic political culture. But from the perspective of a central power ... what is wanted is an idealized subject of a different sort, an asocial one who permits an atomized account of human beings to be operationalized ... A society of such isolated subjects will be more efficiently and pliably governable.

Although the primary responsibility, then, lies with the supply side, at the same time, as consumers and producers we must appreciate we are part of

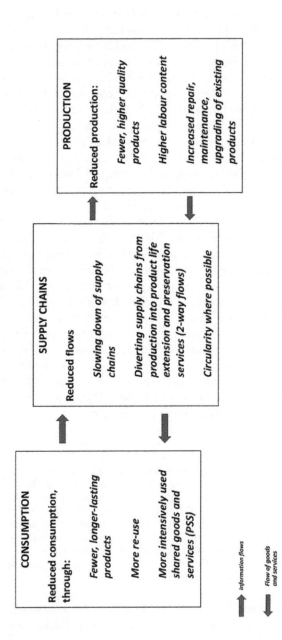

Figure 23.1a   Towards sustainable consumption, production and supply chains/webs

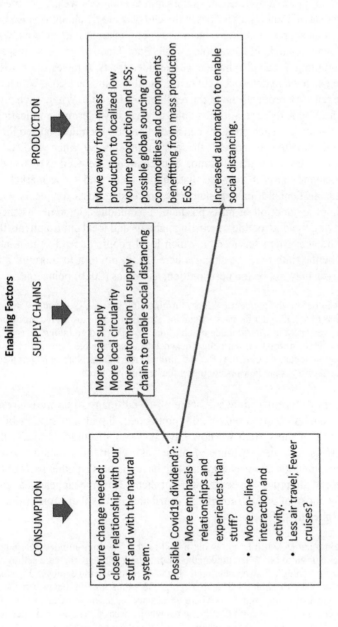

Enabling Factors

CONSUMPTION

Culture change needed: closer relationship with our stuff and with the natural system.

Possible Covid19 dividend?:
- More emphasis on relationships and experiences than stuff?
- More on-line interaction and activity.
- Less air travel; Fewer cruises?

SUPPLY CHAINS

More local supply
More local circularity
More automation in supply chains to enable social distancing

PRODUCTION

Move away from mass production to localized low volume production and PSS; possible global sourcing of commodities and components benefitting from mass production EoS.

Increased automation to enable social distancing.

Figure 23.1b   Towards sustainable consumption, production and supply chains/webs – enabling factors

a system. For example, as consumers in rich countries we are not merely recipients of goods and services at the end of a supply chain; we also help shape that supply chain. This has various implications that are not always fully appreciated. For example, while Fair Trade is in most respects a good thing, it can also have negative side effects. It raises standards to those expected in developed countries, but this comes at a cost, which can often put such products out of the reach of local people. Where such products are foods that are a local staple, this can have serious implications. Our demand for such products can also often impose industrialised forms of production that are novel in those environments. So, when we discover a new 'superfood' such as quinoa or coconut oil, we need to realise that our demand starts to reshape that supply chain and those markets by increasing demand, raising standards, increasing costs for locals while forcing the adoption of mass production techniques; in some instances, involving the destruction of existing habitats and local environments that provide ecosystem services on which local people depend. Again, now may be the time to make changes here too, as a return to 'normal' after the crisis may not be the best solution, as Lomas (2020) points out:

> Even before the pandemic struck, farming simply wasn't working, with millions of smallholder farmers around the globe struggling to survive. Ironically, the very people who produce much of the world's food go hungry every day. For them, normal means being locked into unsustainable farming methods. Normal means battling the effects of drought and floods. Normal means losing out at every stage in a system that's stacked against them.

A return to 'normal' may suit some of us, but many of us were already losing out. As Morton (2018: 208) points out: 'the idea of sustainability implies that the system we now have is worth sustaining'. Again, this highlights the need to think of ourselves as part of a natural system where our actions, however trivial, can have impacts on other parts of the system without us even being aware of them. This may appear challenging for those of us not brought up in tribal societies, but Morton (2018: 89) argues that:

> Being-connected-to is not as big a deal as the very high-minded eco people make it out to be. When they make it out to be a big deal, they are setting the bar for ecological awareness really high. As though being ecologically aware is like being enlightened, or purifying one's sins, or like being capable of seeing everything and everywhere all at once … since you can't see everywhere at once, you can't ever grasp the whole, because wholes aren't actually like that – they aren't everywhere, they don't fit over everything … ecological

awareness and ecological action are much easier than we have been thinking. You are already having ecological awareness and doing ecological action, even by ignoring or being indifferent to them.

He adds that if you have a pet, you can already relate to other elements of the natural system. While indifference may not prevent us from being part of the system, raising this type of awareness is a core part of the ecological thinking transformation suggested in this book and it can start by being aware that you are part of a local community, a family, that you already relate to animals and plants on a daily basis, etc.

This also involves the need for academia to move to much more of a 'systems thinking' and ecological thinking approach through such measures as interdisciplinary and multidisciplinary thinking, both across disciplines and also within individuals. Existing academic disciplines, particularly in areas like business, are often framed around nineteenth- or twentieth-century thinking and concepts and many are obsolete and unable to meet the needs of twenty-first century sustainable businesses (cf. Nieuwenhuis, 2014: Chapter 15). Much can be learned from exposure to other ways of thinking, as we shift from an economic to an ecological worldview or mindset, as suggested by Krebs (2008). In philosophy, for example, recent work by Goff (2019) argues that the only way to explain consciousness – something philosophy has struggled with for centuries – is to assume it exists in a simple, basic form even at the cellular or molecular level. The implications of this, and also of the work by the Object Oriented Ontology (OOO) school, particularly Morton (2010, 2016, 2018) and Bogost (2012), put a completely different complexion on the way we need to interact, not only with other natural players and elements, but also with the objects we derive from those natural sources. They clarify that the parts are as important as the whole, for example. Wider engagement with and internalising of such ideas could radically change the way we see the world and our place within it. We are at the very early stages of such developments and things could easily go the other way, but the 2020 coronavirus crisis has shown us that if our interactions with other parts of the natural system are not based on respect, nature can come back to bite us in ways that not only affect our very existence as humans but that can also wreak havoc on our economic systems. Surely that should help to concentrate our minds?

References

Abbasi, M. and F. Nilsson (2012), 'Themes and challenges in making supply chains environmentally sustainable', *Supply Chain Management: An International Journal*, 17(5), 517–530.

Ackerman, D. (2014), *The Human Age: The World Shaped by Us*, New York: Norton.

Acquier, A. (2019), 'Okja meets Ellul: nature, culture, and life in the iron cage of the technical system', *M@n@gement*, 22(3), 520–536.

Agyeman, J. (2008), 'Toward a "just" sustainability?', *Journal of Media & Cultural Studies*, 22(6), 751–756.

Agyeman, J., R. Bullard and B. Evans (2002), 'Exploring the nexus: bringing together sustainability, environmental justice and equity', *Space and Polity*, 6(1), 70–90.

Alford, D., P. Sackett and G. Nelder (2000), 'Mass-customisation – an automotive perspective', *International Journal of Production Economics*, 65, 99–11.

Alkon, A. and J. Agyeman (2011), 'Introduction: the food movement as polyculture', in A. Alkon and J. Agyeman (eds), *Cultivating Food Justice: Race, Class, and Sustainability*, Cambridge, MA: MIT Press.

Allen, D. and P. Anderson (1994), 'Consumption and social stratification: Bourdieu's distinction', *Advances in Consumer Research*, 21, 70–74.

Alvord, K. (2000), *Divorce your Car! Ending the Love Affair with the Automobile*, Gabriola Island, BC: New Society Publishers.

Andera, J. (2007), *Driving under the Influence: Strategic Trade Policy and Market Integration in the European Car Industry*, Lund Studies in Economic History 42, Lund: Lund University and Stockholm: Almqvist & Wiksell.

Aoki, K. (2015), 'Labour relations and HRM in the automotive industry: Japanese impacts', in P. Nieuwenhuis and P. Wells (eds), *The Global Automotive Industry*, Cheltenham, UK and Northampton, MA: Edward Elgar.

Ashby, A., M. Leat and M. Hudson-Smith (2012), 'Making connections: a review of supply chain management and sustainability literature', *Supply Chain Management: An International Journal*, 17(5), 497–516.

Ashford, N. (2016), 'De-[constructing] growth', *Sustainability*, 8, 1140.

Atkinson, W., S. Roberts and M. Savage (eds) (2012), *Class Inequality in Austerity Britain: Power, Difference and Suffering*, Basingstoke: Palgrave Macmillan.

Ausubel, J. and P. Waggoner (2008), 'Dematerialization: variety, caution, and persistence', *Proceedings of the National Academy of Sciences of the United States of America*, 105(35), 12774–12779.

Automotive Industries (1926), 'Wilson restrained in steel body suit', *Automotive Industries*, 2 December, 1144.

Automotive Industries (1935a), 'Budd gets die stamping order for Soviet car', *Automotive Industries*, 14 September, 355.

Automotive Industries (1935b), 'Russian "Zis" car an 8-in-line with overhead valves; Budd makes dies', *Automotive Industries*, 23 November, 677.

Awaysheh, A. and R. D. Klassen (2010), 'The impact of supply chain structure on the use of supplier socially responsible practices', *International Journal of Operations & Production Management*, 30(12), 1246–1268.

Badré, P. (1990), *Les Automobiles Hispano Suiza: des origines à 1949*, Pontoise: Edijac.

Balfour, C. (2009), *Bristol Cars: A Very British Story*, Sparkford: Haynes.

Barry, J. (2020), 'A genealogy of economic growth as ideology and Cold War core state imperative', *New Political Economy*, 25(1), 18–29.

Barthes, R. (1972), *Mythologies: Roland Barthes*, New York: Hill and Wang.

Baudrillard, J. (1981), *For a Critique of the Political Economy of the Sign*, New York: Telos Press.

Beck, U. (2010), 'Climate for change, or how to create a green modernity?', *Theory, Culture & Society*, March/May, 27, 254–266.

Beder, S. (2004), 'Consumerism – an historical perspective', *Pacific Ecologist*, 9, 42–48.

Bejan, A. and J. Zane (2012), *Design in Nature: How the Constructal Law Governs Evolution in Biology, Physics, Technology and Social Organization*, New York: Doubleday.

Bellu, R. (1988), *Toutes les Voisin: Les dossiers complets de René Bellu*, Le Conquet: René Bellu.

Belz, F. and K. Peattie (2012), *Sustainability Marketing: A Global Perspective*, Chichester: John Wiley.

Benton, R. (2002), 'Environmental racism, consumption, and sustainability', *Business Ethics Quarterly*, 12(1), 83–98.

Benyus, J. (1997), *Biomimicry: Innovation Inspired by Nature*, New York: HarperCollins.

Berk, G.-P. (2009), *André Levebvre and the Cars He Created for Voisin and Citroën: The Life Story of a Passionate Automotive Pioneer*, Dorchester: Veloce.

Berry, C., N. O'Donovan, D. Bailey et al. (2020), *The Covidist Manifesto Assessing the UK State's Emergency Enlargement*, Manchester: Future Economies.

Besch, M. (2002), 'The Soviet auto industry, 1917 to 1953', *Automotive History Review*, 38, Winter, 44–50.

Blaug, M. (1963), 'A survey of the theory of process-innovations', *Economica*, February, 13–32.

Bly, S., W. Gwozdz and L. Reisch (2015), 'Exit from the high street: an exploratory study of sustainable fashion consumption pioneers', *International Journal of Consumer Studies*, 39(2), March, 125–135.

Bogost, I. (2012), *Alien Phenomenology, or What It's Like to Be a Thing*, Minneapolis, MN: University of Minnesota Press.

Booth, R. (2020), 'UK coronavirus response utterly hypocritical, says UN poverty expert', *The Guardian*, 26 April.

Borgé, J. and N. Viasnoff (1981), *Talbot Automobile: Geschichte einer grossen Europäischen Marke*, Munich: Schrader.

Botkin, D. (2017), *25 Myths that Are Destroying the Environment: What Many Environmentalists Believe and Why They Are Wrong*, Guilford, CT: Taylor Trade.

Bourdieu, P. (1984), *Distinction: A Social Critique of the Judgement of Taste*, London: Routledge.

Bourdieu, P. (1985), 'The market of symbolic goods', *Poetics*, 14, 13–45.

Brabazon, P., B. MacCarthy, A. Woodcock and R. Hawkins (2010), 'Mass customization in the automotive industry: comparing interdealer trading and reconfiguration flexibilities in order fulfillment', *Production and Operations Management*, 19(5), September–October, 489–502.

Bricker, D. and J. Ibbitson (2019), *Empty Planet: The Shock of Global Population Decline*, London: Robinson.

Büchs, M. and M. Koch (2019), 'Challenges for the degrowth transition: the debate about wellbeing', *Futures*, 105, 155–165.

Budd, E. G. (1925), *Report for the Rover Company Ltd*, Philadelphia: E. G. Budd Mfg. Co.

Budd, E. G. (1940), 'Personnel relationships in industry', *Journal of the Franklin Institute*, 229(5), May, 545–565.

Burgess, K., P. J. Singh and R. Koroglu (2006), 'Supply chain management: a structured literature review and implications for future research', *International Journal of Operations & Production Management*, 26(7), 703–729.

Carrier, J. (2010), 'Protecting the environment the natural way: ethical consumption and commodity fetishism', *Antipode*, 42(3), 672–689.

Carter, C. (2018), 'Blood in the soil: the racial, racist, and religious dimensions of environmentalism', in L. Hobgood and W. Bauman (eds), *The Bloomsbury Handbook of Religion and Nature*, London: Bloomsbury Academic.

Carter, C. R. and P. L. Easton (2011), 'Sustainable supply chain management: evolution and future directions', *International Journal of Physical Distribution & Logistics Management*, 41(1), 46–62.

Carter, C. R. and D. S. Rogers (2008), 'A framework of sustainable supply chain management: moving toward new theory', *International Journal of Physical Distribution & Logistics Management*, 38(5), 360–387.

Casey, R. (2008), *The Model T: A Centennial History*, Baltimore, MD: Johns Hopkins University Press.

Castoriadis, C. (2010), *A Society Adrift: Interviews and Debates 1974–1997*, New York: Fordham University Press.

Catton, W. and R. Dunlap (1978), 'Environmental sociology: a new paradigm', *American Sociologist*, 13, 41–49.

Chandler, A. D. (1977), *The Visible Hand: The Managerial Revolution in American Business*, Cambridge, MA: Harvard University Press.

Chandler, A. D. (1990), *Scale and Scope: The Dynamics of Industrial Capitalism*, Cambridge, MA: Harvard University Press.

Chapman, J. (2005), *Emotionally Durable Design: Objects, Experiences & Empathy*, London: Earthscan.

Childerhouse, P. and D. Towill (2000), 'Engineering supply chains to match customer requirements', *Logistics Information Management*, 13(6), 337–345.

Christopher, M. and D. R. Towill (2001), 'An integrated model for the design of agile supply chains', *International Journal of Physical Distribution & Logistics Management*, 31(4), 235–246.

Coase, R. (1988), 'The problem of social cost', *Journal of Law and Economics*, 3, 1–44.

Cohen, Y. (2001), *Organiser à l'aube du taylorisme: la pratique d'Ernest Mattern chez Peugeot, 1906–1919*, Besançon: Presses Universitaires Franc-Comtoises.

Colin, M.-A. (2003), *Delahaye 135*, Boulogne-Billancour: ETAI.

Conway, H. (1987), *Bugatti: Le pur-sang des automobiles*, 4th edition, Sparkford: Haynes.

Cooper, T. (2005), 'Slower consumption: reflections on product life spans and the "throwaway society"', *Journal of Industrial Ecology*, 9(1–2), 51–67.

Cooper, T. (2010), *Longer Lasting Products: Alternatives to the Throwaway Society*, Aldershot: Gower.

Courteault, P. (1991), *Automobiles Voisin, 1919–1958*, London: White Mouse Editions and Paris: E.P.A.

Courtenay, V. R. (1987), *Ideas that Move America ... The Budd Company at 75*, Troy, MI: The Budd Company.

Crawford, M. (2009), *The Case for Working with your Hands: Or Why Office Work Is Bad for Us and Fixing Things Feels Good*, London: Viking.

Crawford, M. (2020), *Why We Drive: On Freedom, Risk and Taking Back Control*, London: Bodley Head.

Czech, B. (2013), *Supply Shock: Economic Growth at the Crossroads and the Steady State Solution*, Gabriola Island, BC: New Society Publishers.

Daly, H. E. (1996), 'Against free trade: neoclassical and steady-state perspectives', in K. Dopfer (ed.), *The Global Dimension of Economic Evolution*, Heidelberg: Physica-Verlag HD, pp. 133–146.

Daly, H. (1999), *Ecological Economics and the Ecology of Economics: Essays in Criticism*, Cheltenham, UK and Northampton, MA: Edward Elgar.

Daninos, J. (1981), *Facel Vega: Excellence – HK500 – Facellia*, Paris: E.P.A.

Daub, C.-H. and R. Ergenzinger (2005), 'Enabling sustainable management through a new multi-disciplinary concept of customer satisfaction', *European Journal of Marketing*, 39(9/10), 998–1012.

David, P. (1975), *Technical Choice, Innovation and Economic Growth*, Cambridge: Cambridge University Press.

De Angelis, M. (2007), *The Beginning of History*, London: Pluto Press.

De Graaf, J., D. Wann and T. Naylor (2001), *Affluenza: The All-Consuming Epidemic*, San Francisco, CA: Berrett, Koehler.

De Saussure, F. (1974), *Course in General Linguistics*, London: Fontana/Collins.

De Steiguer, J. (2006), *The Origins of Modern Environmental Thought*, Tucson, AZ: University of Arizona Press.

Debord, G. (1995), *The Society of the Spectacle*, New York: Zone Books.

Dehaghani, R. and D. Newman (2017), '"We're vulnerable too": an (alternative) analysis of vulnerability within English criminal legal aid and police custody', *Oñati Socio-Legal Series*, 7(6), 1199–1228.

154   *Sustainable consumption, production and supply chain management*

Demaria, F., F. Schneider, F. Sekulova and J. Martinez-Alier (2013), 'What is degrowth? From an activist slogan to a social movement', *Environmental Values*, 22(2), 191–215.

Demoulin, F. (2000), *Portraits de Facel: une étoile de l'automobile à Colombes*, Colombes: Musée d'Art et d'Histoire de Colombes.

Denegri-Knott, J., E. Nixon and K. Abraham (2018), 'Politicising the study of sustainable living practices', *Consumption, Markets & Culture*, available at https://doi.org/10.1080/10253866.2017.1414048 [accessed 17 July 2020].

Denning, S. (2013), 'The origin of "the world's dumbest idea": Milton Friedman', *Forbes*, 26 June, available at http://onforb.es/1aeGGWp [accessed 17 July 2020].

Deutsch, C. (1994), *Abschied vom Wegwerfprinzip: Die Wende zur Langlebigkeit in der industriellen Produktion*, Stuttgart: Schaeffer-Poeschel.

Diamond, J. (2005), *Collapse: How Societies Choose to Fail or Survive*, London: Penguin.

Dicken, P. (2007), *Global Shift: Mapping the Changing Contours of the World Economy*, London: SAGE Publications Ltd.

Dietz, R. and D. O'Neill (2013), *Enough Is Enough: Building a Sustainable Economy in a World of Finite Resources*, Abingdon, Oxon: Routledge.

Dodds, A., J. Lawrence and J. Valsiner (1997), 'The personal and the social: Mead's theory of the "generalised other"', *Theory & Psychology*, August, 483–503.

Dolan, P. (2002), 'The sustainability of "sustainable consumption"', *Journal of Macromarketing*, 22(2), 170–181.

Doran, D., A. Hill, K.-S. Hwang and G. Jacob (2007), 'Supply chain modularization: cases from the French automobile industry', *International Journal of Production Economics*, 106, 2–11.

Dorizon, J., F. Peigney and J.-P. Dauliac (1995), *Delahaye: Le Grand Livre*, Paris: EPA.

Dorling, D. (2020), *Slowdown: The End of the Great Acceleration – and Why It's Good for the Planet, the Economy and Our Lives*, New Haven, CT: Yale University Press.

Dosi, G. (1982), 'Technological paradigms and technological trajectories: a suggested interpretation of the determinants and directions of technical change', *Research Policy*, 11, 147–162.

Duncan, J. (2008), *Any Colour – So Long as It's Black: Designing the Model T Ford, 1906–1908*, Auckland: Exisle.

Eckermann, E. (1989), *Technikgeschichte im Deutschen Museum: Automobile*, Munich: Beck & Deutsches Museum.

Ehrenfeld, J. (2009), *Sustainability by Design: A Subversive Strategy for Transforming our Consumer Culture*, New Haven, CT: Yale University Press.

Ehrenfeld, J. R. and A. J. Hoffman (2013), *Flourishing: A Frank Conversation about Sustainability*, Redwood City, CA: Stanford University Press.

Elgin, D. and A. Mitchell (1977), 'Voluntary simplicity: lifestyle of the future?', *The Futurist*, 11, 200–261.

Engels, F. (1974), *Dialectics of Nature*, Moscow: The Marxist-Leninist Library.

Etzioni, A. (1998), 'Voluntary simplicity: a new social movement?', in W. Halal and K. Taylor (eds), *Twenty-First Century Economics*, New York: St Martin's Press, pp. 107–128.

Fabbe-Costes, N., C. Roussat and J. Colin (2011), 'Future sustainable supply chains: what should companies scan?', *International Journal of Physical Distribution & Logistics Management*, 41(3), 228–252.

Feitzinger, E. and H. L. Lee (1997), 'Mass customization at Hewlett-Packard: the power of postponement', *Harvard Business Review*, 75(1), 116–121.

Field, J. and E. Conn (2007), 'The human world seen as living systems', in J. Bryant, M. Atherton and M. Collins (eds), *Design and Information in Biology: From Molecules to Systems*, Design and Nature, Vol. 2, Southampton: WIT Press, pp. 327–344.

Fine, B. and E. Leopold (1993), *The World of Consumption*, London: Routledge.

Fineman, M. A. (2008), 'The vulnerable subject: anchoring equality in the human condition', *Yale Journal of Law and Feminism*, 20(1), 1–23.

Fineman, M. A. (2010), 'The vulnerable subject and the responsive state', *Emory Law Journal*, 60, Emory Public Law Research Paper, 10–130.

Fineman, M. A. (2013), 'Equality, autonomy, and the vulnerable subject in law and politics', in M. Fineman and A. Grear (eds), *Gender in Law, Culture, and Society: Vulnerability: Reflections on a New Ethical Foundation for Law and Politics*, Farnham: Ashgate, pp. 12–28.

Flink, J. J. (1988), *The Automobile Age*, Cambridge, MA, MIT Press.

Follows, S. and D. Jobber (2000), 'Environmentally responsible purchase behaviour: a test of a consumer model', *European Journal of Marketing*, 34(5/6), 723–746.

Ford, H. with S. Crowther (1924), *My Life & Work*, 2nd edition, Heinemann: London.

Ford Motor Co. (1929), *A Tour of the Remarkable Ford Industries during the Days When the End Product Was the Matchless Model A; with 150 photographs*, republished 1961, Arcadia, CA: Post Motor Books.

Foster, P. (2017), *Packard: An Illustrated History 1899–1958*, Pepin, WI: Enthusiast Books.

Fouquet-Hatevilain, P. (1983), *La Fabuleuse aventure d'Hotchkiss 1904–1954*, Pontoise: Edijac.

Fouquet-Hatevilain, P. (1986), *Toute l'histoire Salmson*, Paris: EPA.

Fouquet-Hatevilain, P. (1995), *Album Hotchkiss*, Paris: EPA.

Francis, B. and R. Read (2016), 'Peak stuff: the "growth" party is over. So what next?', *The Ecologist*, 22 January.

Franz, K. (2005), *Tinkering: Consumers Reinvent the Early Automobile*, Philadelphia, PA: University of Pennsylvania Press.

Freeman, C. and F. Louçã (2001), *As Time Goes by: From the Industrial Revolution to the Information Revolution*, Oxford University Press: Oxford.

Freund, P. and G. Martin (1993), *The Ecology of the Automobile*, Montreal: Black Rose.

Friedman, M. (1970), 'The social responsibility of business is to increase its profits', *The New York Times Magazine*, 13 September, www.colorado.edu/

156   *Sustainable consumption, production and supply chain management*

studentgroups/libertarians/issues/friedman-soc-resp-business.html. [page no longer active, but see Denning, 2013].

Frosch, R. and N. Gallopoulos (1989), 'Strategies for manufacturing', *Scientific American*, 261(3), 144–152.

Fujimoto, T. and Y.-W. Park (2014), 'Balancing supply chain competitiveness and robustness through "virtual duel [*sic*] sourcing": lessons from the Great East Japan Earthquake', *International Journal of Production Economics*, 147, 429–436.

Garmestani, A., G. Allen, J. Mittelstaedt, C. Stow and W. Ward (2006), 'Firm size diversity, functional richness, and resilience', *Environment and Development Economics*, 11, 533–551.

Geels, F. (2002), 'Technological transitions as evolutionary reconfiguration processes: a multi-level perspective and a case study', *Research Policy*, 31(8/9), 1257–1274.

Geels, F., R. Kemp, G. Dudley and G. Lyons (2012), *Automobility in Transition? A Socio-Technical Analysis of Sustainable Transport*, Routledge Studies in Sustainability Transition, London: Routledge.

Geels, F., A. McMeekin, J. Mylan and D. Southerton (2015), 'A critical appraisal of sustainable consumption and production research: the reformist, revolutionary and reconfiguration positions', *Global Environmental Change*, 34, 1–12.

General Motors (undated, 1926?), *Fisher Body – Its Contribution to the Automobile Industry*, Detroit: General Motors.

General Motors (1965), *The Story of Fisher Body*, 3rd edition, Detroit: General Motors.

Geng, Y. and R. Côté (2007), 'Diversity in industrial ecosystems', *International Journal of Sustainable Development & World Ecology*, 14, 329–335.

Georgescu-Roegen, N., J. Grinevald and I. Rens (1979), *Demain la Décroissance: Entropie–écologie–économie*, Lausanne: Favre.

Gibson-Graham, J. K. (1996), *The End of Capitalism (as We Knew It): A Feminist Critique of Political Economy*, Oxford: Blackwell.

Gibson-Graham, J. K. (2006), *Postcapitalist Politics*, Minneapolis, MN: University of Minnesota Press.

Gimpel, J. (1976), *The Medieval Machine: The Industrial Revolution in the Middle Ages*, London: Pimlico.

Gladwin, T. N., J. J. Kennelly and T. S. Krause (1995), 'Shifting paradigms for sustainable development: implications for management theory and research', *The Academy of Management Review*, 20(4): 874–907.

Goff, P. (2019), *Galileo's Error: Foundations for a New Science of Consciousness*, London: Rider.

Gold, S., S. Seuring and P. Beske (2010), 'Sustainable supply chain management and inter-organizational resources: a literature review', *Corporate Social Responsibility and Environmental Management*, 17(4), 230–245.

Göpel, M. (2016), *The Great Mindshift: How a New Economic Paradigm and Sustainability Transformations Go Hand in Hand*, Cham, Switzerland: Springer Nature.

Gordon, H. S. (1954), 'The economic theory of a common property resource: The Fishery', *Journal of Political Economy*, 62, 124–142.

Gordon, H. S. (1958), 'Economics and the conservation question', *Journal of Law and Economics*, 1(1), 110–121.

Grayson, S. (1978), 'The all-steel world of Edward Budd', *Automobile Quarterly*, XVI(4), Fourth Quarter, 352–367.

Green, J. (1977), *The Legendary Hispano Suiza*, London: Dalton Watson.

Gruner, R. and D. Power (2017), 'Mimicking natural ecosystems to develop sustainable supply chains: a theory of socio-ecological intergradation', *Journal of Cleaner Production*, 149, 251–264.

Gunderson, L., C. Holling and S. Light (1995), 'Barriers broken and bridges built', in L. Gunderson, C. Holling and S. Light (eds), *Barriers and Bridges to the Renewal of Ecosystems and Institutions*, New York: Columbia University Press.

Haglund, R. (2001), 'Tell-all tome: GM-published history includes company's woes', book review reprinted from *The Flint Journal* in *Society of Automotive Historians Journal*, 191, March–April, 8.

Hahn, T., F. Figge, J. Aragon-Correa and S. Sharma (2017), 'Advancing research on corporate sustainability: off to pastures new or back to the roots?', *Business & Society*, 56(2), 155–185.

Hajer, M. A. (1997), *The Politics of Environmental Discourse: Ecological Modernization and the Policy Process*, Oxford: Oxford University Press.

Hamilton, C. (2003), *Growth Fetish*, Sydney: Allen & Unwin.

Hardin, G. (1968), 'The tragedy of the commons', *Science*, 162, 1243–1248.

Hart, S. L. (1995), 'A natural resource-based view of the firm', *Academy of Management Review*, 20(4), 986–1014.

Hart, S. (1997), 'Beyond greening: strategies for a sustainable world', *Harvard Business Review*, January–February, 66–76.

Hartmann, P. and V. Apaolaza-Ibáñez (2013), 'Desert or rain: standardisation of green advertising versus adaptation to the target audience's natural environment', *European Journal of Marketing*, 47(5/6), 917–933.

Harvey, C. (1981), *The Classic Jaguar Saloons, A Collector's Guide*, London: Motor Racing Publications.

Harvey, D. (2020), 'We need a collective response to the collective dilemma of coronavirus', *Jacobin*, 24 April.

Hawken, P., A. B. Lovins and L. H. Lovins (1999), *Natural Capitalism: The Next Industrial Revolution*, London: Earthscan.

Heeres, R., W. Vermeulen and F. de Walle (2004), 'Eco-industrial park initiatives in the USA and the Netherlands: first lessons', *Journal of Cleaner Production*, 12(8–10), October–December, 985–995.

Helper, S. and M. Sako (2010), 'Management innovation in supply chain: appreciating Chandler in the twenty-first century', *Industrial and Corporate Change*, 19(2), 399–429.

Hickel, J. (2019), 'Degrowth: a theory of radical abundance', *Real-World Economics Review*, 87, 54–68.

Hodgson, G. M. (1992), 'Thorstein Veblen and post-Darwinian economics', *Cambridge Journal of Economics*, 16(3), 285–301.

Hoejmose, S. U. and A. J. Adrien-Kirby (2012), 'Socially and environmentally responsible procurement: a literature review and future research agenda of a managerial issue in the 21st century', *Journal of Purchasing and Supply Management*, 18(4), 232–242.

Hoekstra, S. and J. Romme (1992), *Integrated Logistics Structures: Developing Customer Oriented Goods Flow*, London: McGraw-Hill.

Holdsworth, C. and D. Morgan (2007), 'Revisiting the generalised other: an exploration', *Sociology*, 41(3), 401–417.

Holling, C. (1986), 'The resilience of terrestrial ecosystems: local surprise and global change', in W. Clark and R. Munn (eds), *Sustainable Development of the Biosphere*, Cambridge: Cambridge University Press.

Holloway, J. (2010), *Crack Capitalism*, London: Pluto Press.

Holmes, B. (2013), 'Sea urchins may do swimmingly in acid oceans', *New Scientist*, 2912, 13 April, 12.

Holmström, J., M. Holweg, H. S. Khajavi and J. Partanen (2016), 'The direct digital manufacturing (r)evolution: definition of a research agenda', *Operations Management Research*, 9(1), 1–10.

Holweg, M. and F. Pil (2004), *The Second Century: Reconnecting Customer and Value Chain through Build-to-Order*, Cambridge, MA: MIT Press.

Hounshell, D. (1984), *From the American System to Mass Production, 1800–1932: The Development of Manufacturing Technology in the United States*, Baltimore, MD: Johns Hopkins University Press.

Huber, P. and M. Mills (2005), *The Bottomless Well: The Twilight of Fuel, the Virtue of Waste and Why We Will Never Run Out of Energy*, New York: Basic Books.

Hyde, C. (2005), *The Dodge Brothers: The Men, The Motor Cars, and the Legacy*, Detroit, MI: Wayne State University Press.

Jackson, D. (2011), *What Is an Innovation Ecosystem?* Arlington, VA: National Science Foundation, available at https://erc-assoc.org/sites/default/files/topics/policy_studies/DJackson_Innovation%20Ecosystem_03-15-11.pdf [accessed 17 July 2020].

Jackson, T. (2006), 'Consuming paradise? Towards a social and cultural psychology of sustainable consumption', in T. Jackson (ed.), *The Earthscan Reader in Sustainable Consumption*, London: Earthscan.

Jackson, T. (2009), *Prosperity without Growth: The Transition to a Sustainable Economy*, London: Earthscan.

Jeal, M. (2012), 'Mass confusion: the beginnings of the volume-production of motorcars', *Automotive History Review*, 54, Autumn, 34–47.

Jeffries, M. (1997), *Biodiversity and Conservation*, London: Routledge.

Kallis, G., C. Kerschner and J. Martinez-Alier (2012), 'The economics of degrowth', *Ecological Economics*, 84, 172–180.

Kallis, G., V. Kostakis, S. Lange, B. Muraca, S. Paulson and M. Schmelzer (2018), 'Research on degrowth', *Annual Review of Environment and Resources*, 43, 291–316.

Kaplow, L. (2009), 'Utility from accumulation', NBER Working Paper 15595, Cambridge, MA: NBER.

Kilbourne, W. and S. Beckmann (1998), 'Review and critical assessment of research on marketing and the environment', *Journal of Marketing Management*, 14(6), 513–532.

Kohak, E. (1985), 'Creation's orphans: toward a metaphysics of artifacts', *The Personalist Forum*, 1, 22–42.

Kong, N., O. Salzamann, U. Steger and A. Ionescu-Somers (2002), 'Moving business/industry towards sustainable consumption: the role of NGOs', *European Management Journal*, 20(2), 109–127.

Korten, D. (1995), *When Corporations Rule the World*, London: Earthscan.

Korten, D. (1998), *The Post-Corporate World: Life after Capitalism*, West Hartford, CT: Kumarian Press.

Kostecki, M. (ed.) (1998), *The Durable Use of Consumer Products: New Options for Business and Consumption*, Dordrecht: Kluwer.

Krebs, C. (2008), *The Ecological World View*, Collingwood, Australia: CSIRO Publishing.

Krishnamurthy, R. and C. A. Yauch (2007), 'Leagile manufacturing: a proposed corporate infrastructure', *International Journal of Operations & Production Management*, 27(6), 588–604.

Lamoreaux, N., D. Raff and P. Temin (2002), *Beyond Markets and Hierarchies: Toward a New Synthesis of American Business History*, Cambridge, MA: National Bureau of Economic Research.

Lang, T. (1999), 'The complexities of globalization: the UK as a case study of tensions within the food system and the challenge to food policy', *Agriculture and Human Values*, 16, 169–185.

Latouche, S. (2009), *Farewell to Growth*, Cambridge: Polity Press.

Laux, J. (1976), *In First Gear: The French Automotive Industry to 1914*, Liverpool: Liverpool University Press.

Lebel, L. and S. Lorek (2008), 'Enabling sustainable production–consumption systems', *Annual Review of Environment and Resources*, 33, 241–275.

Lévêque, Ch. and J.-C. Mounolou (2001), *Biodiversité. Dynamique biologique et conservation*, translated into English by Vivien Reuter (2003) as *Biodiversity*, Chichester: John Wiley.

Lévi-Strauss, C. (1974), *Structural Anthropology*, New York: Basic Books.

Lewis, J. (2013), *Beyond Consumer Capitalism: Media and the Limits to Imagination*, Cambridge: Polity Press.

Linton, J. D., R. Klassen and V. Jayaraman (2007), 'Sustainable supply chains: an introduction', *Journal of Operations Management*, 25(6), 1075–1082.

Lipton, B. and S. Bhaerman (2011), *Spontaneous Evolution: Our Positive Future and a Way to Get There from Here*, London: Hay House.

Lodziak, C. (2000), 'On explaining consumption', *Capital & Class*, 72, 111–133.

Lomas, P. (2020), Practical Action supporter letter, July, Rugby: Practical Action.

Lottman, H. (2003), *The Michelin Men: Driving an Empire*, London: Tauris.

Loubet, J.-L. (2001), *Histoire de l'Automobile Française*, Paris: Seuil.

Lutz, H. (2020), 'GM takes 3D printing beyond prototypes', *Automotive News Europe*, 22 June, Europe.autonews.com/automakers/gm-takes-3d-printing-beyond-protptypes?utm_source=daily&utm_medium=email&utm_campaign=20200623&utm_content=article-headline [accessed 23 June 2020].

Luxemburg, R. (2004), 'The Junius Pamphlet: the crisis in German social democracy', in P. Hudis and K. Anderson (eds), *The Rosa Luxemburg Reader*, New York: Monthly Review Press.

Mac New, T. (1955) '3000 passenger car chassis frames per day', *Automotive Industries*, 1 June, 48–51.

Malthus, T. (1798), *An Essay on the Principle of Population*, London: John Murray.

Marsden, T., J. Banks and G. Bristow (2000), 'Food supply chain approaches: exploring their role in rural development', *Sociologia ruralis*, 40(4), 424–438.

Mason-Jones, R. and D. R. Towill (1999), 'Using the information decoupling point to improve supply chain performance', *International Journal of Logistics Management*, 10(2), 13–26.

Mason-Jones, R., B. Naylor and D. Towill (2000), 'Engineering the leagile supply chain', *International Journal of Agile Management Systems*, 2(1), 54–61.

Matsuo, H. (2015), 'Implications of the Tohoku earthquake for Toyota's coordination mechanism: supply chain disruption of automotive semiconductors', *International Journal of Production Economics*, 161, 217–227.

Matthews, L., D. Power, A. Touboulic and L. Marques (2016), 'Building bridges: towards alternative theory of sustainable supply chain management', *Journal of Supply Chain Management*, 52(1), 82–94.

Mazzucato, M. (2013), *The Entrepreneurial State: Debunking Public vs. Private Sector Myths*, London: Anthem.

Mazzucato, M. (2019), *The Value of Everything: Making and Taking the Global Economy*, London: Penguin.

McCann, K. (2000), 'The diversity–stability debate', *Nature*, 405, 11 May, 228–233.

McCarthy, L., A. Touboulic and J. Glover (2020), 'Who is milking it? Scripted stories of food labour processes', Working Paper.

McCarthy, L., A. Touboulic and L. Matthews (2018), 'Voiceless but empowered farmers in corporate supply chains: contradictory imagery and instrumental approach to empowerment', *Organization*, 25(5), 609–635.

McCracken, G. (1986), 'Culture and consumption: a theoretical account of the structure and movement of the cultural meaning of consumer goods', *Journal of Consumer Research*, 13, June, 71–84.

McCracken, G. (1988), *Culture and Consumption*, Bloomington, IN: Indiana University Press.

McCracken, G. (2005), *Culture and Consumption II: Markets, Meaning and Brand Management*, Bloomington, IN: Indiana University Press.

McDonagh, P. and A. Prothero (2014), 'Sustainability marketing research: past, present and future', *Journal of Marketing Management*, 30(11–12), 1186–1219.

McDonough, W. and M. Braungart (2002), *Cradle to Cradle: Remaking the Way We Make Things*, New York: North Point Press.

McGouran, C. and A. Prothero (2016), 'Enacted voluntary simplicity – exploring the consequences of requesting consumers to intentionally consume less', *European Journal of Marketing*, 50(1/2), 189–212.

McKenzie, R. (1924), 'The ecological approach to the study of human community', *American Journal of Sociology*, 30(3), November, 287–301.

Mead, G. (1934), *Mind, Self and Society* (1967 edition), Chicago, IL: University of Chicago Press.

Meadows, D. (2009), *Thinking in Systems: A Primer*, London: Earthscan.

Meadows, D., D. Meadows, J. Randers and W. Behrens (1972), *The Limits to Growth*, New York: New American Library.

Meadows, D., J. Randers and D. Meadows (2005), *Limits to Growth: The 30-Year Update*, London: Earthscan.

Mexal, S. (2004), 'Consuming cities: hip hop's urban wilderness and the cult of masculinity', in M. Allister (ed.), *Eco-Man: New Perspectives on Masculinity and Nature*, Charlottesville, VA: University of Virginia Press, pp. 235–247.

Miemczyk, J., T. E. Johnsen and M. Macquet (2012), 'Sustainable purchasing and supply management: a structured literature review of definitions and measures at the dyad, chain and network levels', *Supply Chain Management: An International Journal*, 17(5), 478–496.

Mill, J. S. (1848), *Principles of Political Economy with Some of their Applications to Social Philosophy* (1965 reprint), New York: Kelley.

Miller, D. (ed.) (2001), *Car Cultures*, Oxford: Berg.

Miller, P. (2010), *Smart Swarm*, London: Collins.

Molles, M. (2005), *Ecology, Concepts and Applications*, 3rd edition, New York: McGraw-Hill.

Monbiot, G. (2020), 'Lab-grown food will soon destroy farming – and save the planet', *The Guardian*, 8 January, available at www.theguardian.com/commentisfree/2020/jan/08/lab-grown-food-destroy-farming-save-planet.

Montabon, F., M. Pagell and Z. Wu (2016), 'Making sustainability sustainable', *Journal of Supply Chain Management*, 52(2), 11–27.

Montague of Beaulieu, Baron (1975), *Jaguar*, Foulis mini marque history series, Sparkford: Haynes.

Moore, J. (1993), 'Predators and prey: a new ecology of competition', *Harvard Business Review*, May–June, 75–86.

Moore, J. (1997), *The Death of Competition*, New York: HarperBusiness.

Moore, J. (2006), 'Business ecosystems and the view from the firm', *The Antitrust Bulletin*, 51(1), 31–75.

Morton, T. (2010), *The Ecological Thought*, Cambridge, MA: Harvard University Press.

Morton, T. (2016), *Dark Ecology: For a Logic of Future Coexistence*, New York: Columbia University Press.

Morton, T. (2018), *Being Ecological*, London: Pelican.

Motor (1937), 'Trend toward frameless cars', *Motor*, 2, 126.

Moyano-Fuentes, J. and M. Sacristán-Díaz (2012), 'Learning on lean: a review of thinking and research', *International Journal of Operations & Production Management*, 32(5), 551–582.

Muis, H. (2006), 'Eternally yours: some theory and practice on cultural sustainable product development', in P. Verbeek and P. Slob (eds), *User Behaviour and Technology Development: Shaping Sustainable Relations between Consumers and Technologies*, Frankfurt: Springer, pp. 277–293.

Naylor, J. B., M. Naim and D. Berry (1999), 'Leagility: integrating the lean and agile manufacturing paradigms in the total supply chain', *International Journal of Production Economics*, 62(1–2), 107–118.

162   *Sustainable consumption, production and supply chain management*

Neale, J. (2008), *Stop Global Warming: Change the World*, London: Bookmarks Publications.
Nelson, R. R. and S. G. Winter (1982), *An Evolutionary Theory of Economic Change*, Cambridge, MA: The Belknap Press.
Newman, D. (2013), 'Cars and consumption', *Capital & Class*, 37(3), 454–473.
Newman, D. (2014), 'South Park and social research: what cartoons can tell us about sustainable mobility', *Journal of Popular Television*, 2(2), 173–188.
Newman, D. (2017), 'Automobiles and socioeconomic sustainability: do we need a mobility bill of rights?', *Transfers*, 7(2), 100–106.
Nieuwenhuis, P. (1994), 'The long-life car: investigating a motor industry heresy', in P. Nieuwenhuis and P. Wells (eds), *Motor Vehicles in the Environment: Principles and Practice*, Chichester: John Wiley & Sons, pp. 153–172.
Nieuwenhuis, P. (2008), 'From banger to classic – a model for sustainable car consumption?', *International Journal of Consumer Studies*, 32(6), November, 648–655.
Nieuwenhuis, P. (2014), *Sustainable Automobility: Understanding the Car as a Natural System*, Cheltenham, UK and Northampton, MA: Edward Elgar.
Nieuwenhuis, P. (2018a), 'Micro-factory retailing: an alternative, more sustainable business model', *IEEE-EMR*, 46(1), 39–46.
Nieuwenhuis, P. (2018b), 'Alternative business models and entrepreneurship: the case of electric vehicles', *International Journal of Entrepreneurship and Innovation*, 19(1), 33–45.
Nieuwenhuis, P. and E. Katsifou (2015), 'More sustainable automotive production through understanding decoupling points in leagile manufacturing', *Journal of Cleaner Production*, 95, 232–241; doi.org/10/1016/jclepro2015.02.084.
Nieuwenhuis, P. and C. Lämmgård (2013), 'Industrial ecology as an ecological model for business: diversity and firm survival', *Progress in Industrial Ecology – An International Journal*, 8(3), 189–204; doi: 10.1504/PIE.2013.060672.
Nieuwenhuis, P. and P. Wells (1997), *The Death of Motoring? Car Making and Automobility in the 21st Century*, Chichester: John Wiley.
Nieuwenhuis, P. and P. Wells (2003), *The Automotive Industry and the Environment – A Technical, Business and Social Future*, Cambridge: Woodhead and Boca Raton, FL: CRC Press.
Nieuwenhuis, P. and P. Wells (2007), 'The all-steel body as a cornerstone to the foundations of the mass production car industry', *Industrial and Corporate Change*, 16(2), 183–211; doi:10.1093/icc/dtm001.
Nieuwenhuis, P. and P. Wells (2009), *Car Futures: Rethinking the Automotive Industry beyond the American Model*, Westbury: Trend Tracker, available at www.trendtracker.co.uk.
Nieuwenhuis, P. and P. Wells (eds) (2015), *The Global Automotive Industry*, Chichester: John Wiley & Sons.
Odum, E. (1959), *Fundamentals of Ecology*, Philadelphia, PA and London: W. B. Saunders.
Orsato, R. (2009), *Sustainability Strategies: When Does It Pay to Be Green?* London: Palgrave Macmillan.

Pagell, M. and A. Shevchenko (2014), 'Why research in sustainable supply chain management should have no future', *Journal of Supply Chain Management*, 50(1), 44–55.

Park-Poaps, H. and K. Rees (2010), 'Stakeholder forces of socially responsible supply chain management orientation', *Journal of Business Ethics*, 92(2), 305–322.

Parsons, D. (2002), 'The Sustainability of Alternative Economic Theories: The British Luxury Specialist Car Manufacturing Sector & Bristol Cars Ltd', unpublished MBA dissertation, Cardiff University.

Pascal, D. (1998), *Auto Passion Auto Collection No 48: Facel Vega*, Saint Cloud: Michel Hommel.

Paulraj, A. (2011), 'Understanding the relationships between internal resources and capabilities, sustainable supply management and organizational sustainability', *Journal of Supply Chain Management*, 47(1), 19–37.

Pearce, D. (1993), *Economic Values and the Natural World*, London: Earthscan.

Pearce, D., A. Markandya and E. Barbier (1989), *Blueprint for a Green Economy*, London: Earthscan.

Peattie, K. (2011), 'Developing and delivering social science research for sustainability', in A. Franklin and P. Blyton, *Researching Sustainability: A Guide to Social Science Methods, Practice and Engagement*, Abingdon: Earthscan, pp. 54–70.

Perrings, C. (1998), 'Resilience in the dynamics of economy–environment systems', *Environmental and Resource Economics*, 11(3–4), 503–520.

Peterson, G. (2000), 'Political ecology and ecological resilience: an integration of human and ecological dynamics', *Ecological Economics*, 35, 323–336.

Peterson, G., C. Allen and C. Holling (1998), 'Ecological resilience, biodiversity, and scale', *Ecosystems*, 1, 6–18.

Pigou, A. (1920), *The Economics of Welfare*, London: Macmillan.

Piketty, T. (2013), *Capital in the Twenty-First Century*, Cambridge, MA: Harvard University Press.

Porsche (1976), *Long-Life Car Research Project*: Final Report Phase I: Summary. Stuttgart: Dr Ing. h.c. F. Porsche AG.

Preuss, L. (2005), 'Rhetoric and reality of corporate greening: a view from the supply chain management function', *Business Strategy and the Environment*, 14(2), 123–139.

Provan, K. and A. Fish (2007), 'Interorganizational networks at the network level: a review of the empirical literature on whole networks', *Journal of Management*, 33(2), June, 479–516.

Purdy, J. (2019), *This Land Is Our Land: The Struggle for a New Commonwealth*, Princeton, NJ: Princeton University Press.

Quarrie, J. (ed.) (1992), *Earth Summit 1992: The United Nations Conference on Environment and Development, Rio de Janeiro 1992*, London: The Regency Press.

Raff, D. (1991), 'Making cars and making money in the interwar automobile industry: economies of scale and scope and the manufacturing behind the marketing', *Business History Review*, Winter, 721–753.

Raff, D. (1994), 'Models of the evolution of production systems and the diffusion of mass production methods in the American motor vehicles industry', paper presented at the 2nd International Meeting of GERPISA, Paris, June.

Ram, A. and R. Milne (2016), 'Ikea senses room to grow amid "peak stuff"', *Financial Times*, 18 January.

Ramirez, E., F. Jiménez and R. Gau (2015), 'Concrete and abstract goals associated with the consumption of environmentally sustainable products', *European Journal of Marketing*, 49(9/10), 1645–1665.

Reardon, S. (2013), 'Stone tools helped shape our hands', *New Scientist*, 2912, 13 April, 11.

Renou, M. (1984), *Toute l'Histoire Facel Vega*, E.P.A.: Paris.

Reynolds, J. (1996), *André Citroën: The Man and the Motor Cars*, Stroud: Wren's Park.

Rivera-Camino, J. (2007), 'Re-evaluating green marketing strategy: a stakeholder perspective', *European Journal of Marketing*, 41(11/12), 1328–1358.

Riversimple (2017), www.riversimple.com/how-the-business-works/ [accessed 17 July 2020].

Rockström, J., W. Steffen, K. Noone et al. (2009), 'Planetary boundaries: exploring the safe operating space for humanity', *Ecology and Society*, 14(2), 32, available at www.ecologyandsociety.org/vol14/iss2/art32/ [accessed 17 July 2020].

Rosenberg, N. (1979), 'Technological interdependence in the American economy', *Technology and Culture*, January, 25–50.

Rosenberg, N. (1982), *Exploring the Black Box: Technology and Economics*, Cambridge: Cambridge University Press.

Rousseau, J. (1978), *Les Automobiles Delage*, Paris: Larivière.

Ruddiman, W. (2005), *Plows, Plagues and Petroleum: How Humans Took Control of Climate*, Princeton, NJ: Princeton University Press.

Sabatès, F. (1986), *Les Voitures Françaises 1950–1955*, Collection auto archives No 12, Levallois-Perret : Edition Nationale 7.

Sabel, C. and J. Zeitlin (1985), 'Historical alternatives to mass production: politics, markets and technology in nineteenth-century industrialisation', *Past and Present*, 108, August, 133–176.

Sabel, C. and J. Zeitlin (1997), *World of Possibilities: Studies in Modern Capitalism/Etudes sur le Capitalisme Moderne*, Cambridge: Cambridge University Press and Paris: Maison des Sciences de l'Homme.

Said, E. (1995), *Orientalism*, Harmondsworth: Penguin.

Sanne, C. (2002), 'Willing consumers – or locked-in? Policies for a sustainable consumption', *Ecological Economics*, 42(1–2), August, 273–287.

Sarkis, A. (2017), 'A comparative study of theoretical behaviour change models predicting empirical evidence for residential energy conservation behaviours', *Journal of Cleaner Production*, 141, 526–537.

Schneider, F., G. Kallisa, and J. Martinez-Alier (2010), 'Crisis or opportunity? Economic degrowth for social equity and ecological sustainability. Introduction to this special issue', *Journal of Cleaner Production*, 8, 511–518.

Schumacher, E. (1973), *Small Is Beautiful: A Study of Economics as if People Mattered*, London: Sphere.

Schumpeter, J. (1942), *Capitalism, Socialism, and Democracy*, New York: Harper & Brothers.

Schweitzer, S. (1982), *Des Engrenages à la chaine: les usines Citroën, 1915–1935*, Lyon: Presses Universitaires.

Schwenkenbecher, A. (2014), 'Is there an obligation to reduce one's individual carbon footprint?', *Critical Review of International Social and Political Philosophy*, 17(2), 168–188.

Sedgwick, M. (1973), *Cars in Profile No 7: Facel Vega*, Windsor: Profile Publications.

Seuring, S., J. Sarkis, M. Müller and P. Rao (2008), 'Sustainability and supply chain management: an introduction to the special issue', *Journal of Cleaner Production*, 16(15), 1545–1551.

Shaw, D., T. Newholm and R. Dickinson (2006), 'Consumption as voting: an exploration of consumer empowerment', *European Journal of Marketing*, 40(9/10), 1049–1067.

Sheller, M. (2004), 'Automotive emotions: feeling the car', *Theory, Culture & Society*, 21(4/5), 221–242.

Shireman, W. (2001), quoted in 'Business as a living system: the value of industrial ecology', editorial, *California Management Review*, 43(3), 16–25.

Shrivastava, P. (1995), 'The role of corporations in achieving ecological sustainability', *Academy of Management Review*, 20(4), 936–960.

Simpson, D. F. and D. J. Power (2005), 'Use the supply relationship to develop lean and green suppliers', *Supply Chain Management: An International Journal*, 10(1), 60–68.

Smith, B. (1980), *The Daimler Tradition*, Isleworth: Transport Bookman.

Sonnino, R. and T. Marsden (2006), 'Beyond the divide: rethinking relationships between alternative and conventional food networks in Europe', *Journal of Economic Geography*, 6(2), 181–199.

Soron, D. (2009), 'Driven to drive: cars and the problem of "compulsory" consumption', in J. Conley and A. McLaren (eds), *Car Trouble: Critical Studies of Automobility*, Farnham: Ashgate, pp. 181–198.

Spaargaren, G. (2003), 'Sustainable consumption: a theoretical and environmental policy perspective', *Society and Natural Resources*, 16, 687–701.

Sperling, D. (2018), *Three Revolutions: Steering Automated, Shared, and Electric Vehicles to a Better Future*, Washington, DC: Island Press.

Spiro, J. (2009), *Defending the Master Race: Conservation, Eugenics, and the Legacy of Madison Grant*, Burlington, VT: University of Vermont Press.

Spitz, A. (1983), *Talbot: des Talbot-Darracq aux Talbot-Lago*, Paris: E.P.A.

Spyker, S. (2007), *Technology & Spirituality: How the Information Revolution Affects our Spiritual Lives*, Woodstock, VT: Skylight Paths.

Stahel, W. (1998), 'Product durability and re-take after use', in M. Kostecki (ed.), *The Durable Use of Consumer Products: New Options for Business and Consumption*, Dordrecht: Kluwer.

Stahel, W. (2016), 'The circular economy', *Nature*, 531(7595), 23 March, 435–438; doi: 10.1038/531435a, available at www.nature.com/news/the-circular-economy-1.19594 [accessed 18 June 2020].

Stamets, P. (2005), *Mycelium Running: How Mushrooms Can Help Save the World*, Berkeley, CA: Ten Speed Press.
Starik, M. (1995), 'Should trees have managerial standing? Toward stakeholder status for non-human nature', *Journal of Business Ethics*, 14(3), 207–217.
Starik, M. and G. P. Rands (1995), 'Weaving an integrated web: multilevel and multisystem perspectives of ecologically sustainable organizations', *The Academy of Management Review*, 20(4), 908–935.
Stavrakakis, Y. (2006), 'Objects of consumption, causes of desire: consumerism and advertising in societies of commanded enjoyment', *Gramma*, 14, 83–106.
Steinhilper, R. (1998), *Remanufacturing: The Ultimate Form of Recycling*, Stuttgart: Fraunhofer IRB.
Tate, W. L., L. M. Ellram and J. F. Kirchoff (2010), 'Corporate social responsibility reports: a thematic analysis related to supply chain management', *Journal of Supply Chain Management*, 46(1), 19–44.
Taylor, J. (1994), *Classic Citroëns, Vol. 1: Traction Avant 1934–1957*, London: Yesteryear Books.
Thornton, L. M., C. W. Autry, D. M. Gligor and A. B. Brik (2013), 'Does socially responsible supplier selection pay off for customer firms? A cross-cultural comparison', *Journal of Supply Chain Management*, 49(3), 66–89.
Thum, E. E. (1928), 'Many advantages realized in body of 5-piece all-steel design', *Automotive Industries*, 15 September, 370–372.
Tilman, D. (2000), 'Causes, consequences and ethics of biodiversity', *Nature*, 405, 11 May, 208–211.
Todd, D. (2012), 'You are what you buy: postmodern consumerism and the construction of self', *University of Hawai'i at Hilo: Hawai'i Community College HOHONU*, 10, 48–50.
Touboulic, A. and H. Walker (2015), 'Theories in sustainable supply chain management: a structured literature review', *International Journal of Physical Distribution & Logistics Management*, 45(1/2), 16–42.
Trainer, E. (2014), 'The "simple life" manifesto and how it could save us', *The Conversation*, 28 December, available at www.theconversation.com/the-simple-life-manifesto-and-how-it-could-save-us-33081 [accessed 17 July 2020].
Tregidga, H., M. Milne and K. Kearins (2018), 'Ramping up resistance: corporate sustainable development and academic research', *Business & Society*, 57(2), 292–334.
Tsing, A. (2009), 'Supply chains and the human condition', *Rethinking Marxism*, 21(2), 148–176.
Turnquist, R. (1965), *The Packard Story: The Car and the Company*, Somerville, NJ: Somerset.
Tylecote, A. (1991), *The Long Wave in the World Economy*, Routledge: London.
Tylecote, A. and G. Vertova (2007), 'Technology and institutions in changing specialization: chemicals and motor vehicles in the United States, United Kingdom, and Germany', *Industrial and Corporate Change*, 16(5), 875–911.
UN (2019), Revision of World Population Prospects, available at https://population.un.org/wpp/ [accessed 17 July 2020].
Urry, J. (2011), *Climate Change and Society*, Cambridge: Polity Press.

References 167

Valiorgue, B. and X. Hollandts (2019), 'Combien de fermes de 1000 vaches pour nourrir les Français?', *The Conversation*, 21 February, available at https://theconversation.com/combien-de-fermes-de-1-000-vaches-pour-nourrir-les-francais-111872 [accessed 28 October 2020].

Van Bommel, H. W. (2011), 'A conceptual framework for analyzing sustainability strategies in industrial supply networks from an innovation perspective', *Journal of Cleaner Production*, 19(8), 895–904.

Veblen, T. (1898), 'Why is economics not an evolutionary science?', *Quarterly Journal of Economics*, 12(4), 373–397.

Veblen, T. (1994), *The Collected Works of Thorstein Veblen*, Vol. 1, London: Routledge.

Velliky, J. R. and J. M. Pitrone (1992), *Dodge Brothers/Budd Co. Historical Photo Album*, Detroit, MI: Harlo.

Walker, B. and D. Salt (2006), *Resilience Thinking: Sustaining Ecosystems and People in a Changing World*, Washington, DC: Island Press.

Walker, B., S. Carpenter, J. Anderies et al. (2002), 'Resilience management in social-ecological systems: a working hypothesis for a participatory approach', *Conservation Ecology*, 6(1), 14, available at www.consecol.org/vol6/iss1/art14 [accessed 17 July 2020].

Wang, Z. and J. Sarkis (2013), 'Investigating the relationship of sustainable supply chain management with corporate financial performance', *International Journal of Productivity and Performance Management*, 62(8), 871–888.

Wang, Y., A. Touboulic and M. O'Neill (2018), 'An exploration of solutions for improving access to affordable fresh food with disadvantaged Welsh communities', *European Journal of Operational Research*, 268(3), 1021–1039.

WCED, World Commission on Environment and Development (1987), *Our Common Future*, Oxford: University Press.

Weinert, C. (1957), 'Specialized handling equipment for chassis frame assembly at Budd Co. plant', *Automotive Industries*, 15 October, 48–51.

Wells, P. (2010), *The Automotive Industry in an Era of Eco-Austerity*, Cheltenham, UK and Northampton, MA: Edward Elgar.

Wells, P. (2013), *Business Models for Sustainability*, Cheltenham, UK and Northampton, MA: Edward Elgar.

Wells, P. and A. Morreau (2009), 'UK car market: fragmentation returns in 2009', *Automotive World*, March.

Wells, P. and P. Nieuwenhuis (2000), 'Why big business should think small', *Automotive World*, July/August, 32–38.

Wells, P. and R. Orsato (2005), 'Product, process and structure: redesigning the industrial ecology of the automobile', *The Journal of Industrial Ecology*, 9(3), 1–16.

Wells, P., P. Nieuwenhuis and R. Orsato (2012), 'The nature and causes of inertia in the automotive industry: regime stability and non-change', in F. Geels, R. Kemp, G. Dudley and G. Lyons (eds), *Automobility in Transition? A Socio-Technical Analysis of Sustainable Transport*, Routledge Studies in Sustainability Transition, Vol. 2, New York: Routledge.

Whiteman, G., B. Walker and P. Perego (2013), 'Planetary boundaries: ecological foundations for corporate sustainability', *Journal of Management Studies*, 50(2), March, 307–336.

Wilk, R. (ed.) (2006), *Fast Food/Slow Food: The Cultural Economy of the Global Food System*, Lanham, MD, Altamira.

Williams, K., C. Haslam, S. Johal and J. Williams (1994), *Cars, Analysis, History, Cases*, Providence, RI: Berghahn.

Williams, M. (2016a), 'Kumamoto earthquake disrupts vehicle assembly across Japan', *Automotive Logistics*, 15 April.

Williams, M. (2016b), 'Japanese shockwaves reach North America', *Automotive Logistics*, 28 April.

Williams, M. (2016c), 'Toyota still dealing with parts disruption in Japan', *Automotive Logistics*, 11 May.

Williams, M. (2016d), 'Toyota forced to suspend production in Japan because of steel supply problems', *Automotive Logistics*, 2 February.

Williams, M. (2016e), 'Explosion puts brakes on Toyota assembly', *Automotive Logistics*, 1 June.

Wilson, E. O. (2006), *The Creation*, New York: Norton.

Winn, M. and S. Pogutz (2013), 'Business, ecosystems and biodiversity: new horizons for management research', *Organization & Environment*, 26(2), 203–229.

Wolmar, C. (2018), *Driverless Cars: On a Road to Nowhere*, London: London Publishing Partnership.

Womack, J. and D. Jones (1996), *Lean Thinking: Banish Waste and Create Wealth in Your Corporation*, London: Simon and Schuster.

Womack, J., D. Jones and D. Roos (1990), *The Machine that Changed the World*, New York: Rawson.

Wong, C. W. Y. (2013), 'Leveraging environmental information integration to enable environmental management capability and performance', *Journal of Supply Chain Management*, 49(2), 114–136.

Wynn-Williams, M. (2009), *Surfing the Global Tide: Automotive Giants and How to Survive Them*, Basingstoke: Palgrave-Macmillan.

Yuen, S. (2012), 'The Effects of the Japanese Earthquake and Tsunami on the Toyota Supply Chain', MSc dissertation, Cardiff University.

Zuboff, S. (2019), *The Age of Surveillance Capitalism: The Fight for a Human Future at the New Frontier of Power*, London: Profile.

Index